WeightWatche

CW01670216

five ingredient 15 minute RECIPES

Oxmoor House®

At Your Service

To send a comment or question, write to:
Oxmoor House Special Editions
2100 Lakeshore Drive
Birmingham, AL 35209

Be sure to check with your health-care provider before making any changes in your diet.

INTERESTED IN MORE OXMOOR HOUSE COOKBOOKS?

To learn more about our resources for living a healthy lifestyle, visit **oxmoorhouse.com** and click on our site's "Cooking" link, or call 1-800-491-0551.

To search, savor, and share thousands of recipes, visit **myrecipes.com**

To order additional publications, call 1-800-765-6400.

WEIGHT WATCHERS® ***FIVE INGREDIENT 15 MINUTE RECIPES*** is published by Time Home Entertainment Inc.
135 West 50th Street, New York, NY 10020.

ISBN-13: 978-0-8487-3315-5

ISBN-10: 0-8487-3315-0

WeightWatchers®

five ingredient 15 minute RECIPES

EDITOR Andrea C. Kirkland, M.S., R.D.
PROJECT EDITOR Emily Chappell

OXMOOR HOUSE

VP, PUBLISHING DIRECTOR Jim Childs
EDITORIAL DIRECTOR Susan Payne Dobbs
MANAGING EDITOR Laurie S. Herr
SENIOR EDITOR Heather Averett
DIRECTOR, TEST KITCHENS Elizabeth Tyler Austin
ASSISTANT DIRECTORS, TEST KITCHENS Julie Christopher, Julie Gunter
TEST KITCHENS PROFESSIONALS Wendy Ball, Allison E. Cox, Victoria E. Cox, Margaret Monroe Dickey, Alyson Moreland Haynes, Callie Nash, Kathleen Royal Phillips, Catherine Crowell Steele, Leah Van Deren
PHOTOGRAPHY DIRECTOR Jim Bathie
SENIOR PHOTO STYLIST Kay E. Clarke
ASSOCIATE PHOTO STYLIST Katherine Eckert Coyne
SENIOR PRODUCTION MANAGER Greg A. Amason
CONTRIBUTORS Leigh McIntosh Addington, Susan M. McIntosh, M.S., R.D. (editors); Carol O. Loria (designer and compositor); Carmine Loper (copy editor); Lauren Brooks (proofreader); Elizabeth Nelson, Caitlin Watzke (interns)

TIME HOME ENTERTAINMENT INC.

PUBLISHER Richard Fraiman
GENERAL MANAGER Steven Sandonato
EXECUTIVE DIRECTOR, MARKETING SERVICES Carol Pittard
EXECUTIVE DIRECTOR, RETAIL & SPECIAL SALES Tom Mifsud
DIRECTOR, NEW PRODUCT DEVELOPMENT Peter Harper
ASSISTANT DIRECTOR, NEWSSTAND MARKETING Laura Adam
ASSISTANT DIRECTOR, BRAND MARKETING Joy Butts
ASSOCIATE COUNSEL Helen Wan
BRAND MANAGER Victoria Alfonso
FOR ADVERTISING CONTACT Paul C. Kostial, President
AudienceInnovation.com
888-241-6634, x719

On the front cover: Chicken Scaloppini (page 39)

Kalamata-and-Herbed Cheese Mini Phyllos, page 19

Chicken Cutlets with Fontina and Fresh Blueberry Sauce, page 15

Kale with Cranberries, Apricots, and Almonds, page 71

Flourless Chocolate Cakes, page 87

contents

Beefy Corn and Black Bean Chili, page 62

welcome

A **new year calls for a new beginning and a chance to start a routine** of preparing nutritious everyday meals that you and your family will love. With more than 100 delicious recipes and no-fuss meal ideas, this latest edition of ***Weight Watchers Five Ingredient 15 Minute Recipes*** is just what you need to get on track.

Most busy cooks today want fast, practical meal options that don't require a lot of effort and can help them get in and out of the kitchen quickly. You can do just that with these reliable recipes that have short ingredient lists and easy-to-follow, step-by-step instructions. Each recipe meets at least one of these two criteria: It requires five ingredients or less (excluding water, cooking spray, salt, pepper, and optional ingredients), or it can be whipped up in 15 minutes or less. And many fit the bill for both!

These recipes were designed with you in mind, as each recipe includes the ***PointsPlus***® value per serving, as well as a nutritional analysis. We've even created a special index that groups recipes by ***PointsPlus*** values for your convenience. And if you're looking for recipes that can be made ahead, require no cooking, are portable, or are guaranteed family favorites, we've color-coded these categories in the index so you can find the perfect recipes with ease.

With so many mouthwatering and filling dishes, it's hard to know where to begin. Here are a few of our staff favorites:

- **Beef Tenderloin Steaks with Red Wine-Mushroom Sauce (page 33)**
- **Cheeseburger Penne (page 42)**
- **Spinach-Artichoke Pizza (page 44)**
- **Italian Wedding Soup (page 61)**

Try these decadent desserts that will satisfy your sweet tooth and won't sabotage those New Year's resolutions:

- **Graham Cracker Chocolate Chip Cookies (page 81)**
- **Chocolate Pretzel Bark (page 85)**
- **Brandied Pear Pastries with Apricot Glaze (page 87)**

We hope these easy recipes will bring exciting new possibilities to your dining table, and we wish you all the best in the upcoming year.

The Editors

superfast menus

With streamlined game plans and very simple recipes, these fast and delicious menus enable you to put together any meal with ease.

Easy Lunch Menu

PointsPlus **value per serving: 7**

Tuna and White Bean Salad

Parmesan Toasts

Tuna and White Bean Salad

PointsPlus **value:** 5
PREP: 13 minutes

White balsamic vinegar has a lighter color and flavor than traditional balsamic vinegar. Use white balsamic when additional color is not desired in your dish.

- 2 (6-ounce) cans albacore tuna in water, drained
- 1 (15.5-ounce) can cannellini beans or other white beans, rinsed and drained
- 2 cups grape tomatoes, halved
- 1 medium cucumber, peeled and chopped (2 cups)
- ¼ cup thinly sliced red onion
- 4 cups fresh baby spinach
- 2 tablespoons white balsamic vinegar
- 1 tablespoon fresh lemon juice
- 1 tablespoon olive oil
- ½ teaspoon freshly ground black pepper
- ¼ teaspoon salt

1. Combine all ingredients in a large bowl; toss well. **YIELD:** 4 servings (serving size: 2½ cups).

PER SERVING: CAL 212; FAT 5.2g (sat 0.6g); PRO 21.9g; CARB 21.1g; FIB 5.8g; SUG 3.6g; CHOL 28mg; IRON 3.6mg; SOD 578mg; CALC 105mg

GAME PLAN

1 While broiler preheats:
- Slice bread for toasts.
- Prepare salad.

2 Prepare toasts.

Parmesan Toasts

PointsPlus **value:** 2
PREP: 2 minutes ■ **COOK:** 4 minutes

- 4 (1-ounce) slices diagonally cut multigrain bread baguette (about 1 inch thick)
- Olive oil–flavored cooking spray
- ½ of a garlic clove
- ¼ cup grated Parmigiano-Reggiano cheese
- 1/16 teaspoon freshly ground black pepper

1. Preheat broiler.
2. Place bread slices on a baking sheet. Lightly coat top sides of bread slices with cooking spray. Broil 2 minutes or until golden brown. Turn slices over; broil 1 minute. Remove pan from oven, and gently rub top sides of bread slices with garlic. Sprinkle each slice evenly with 1 tablespoon cheese and ¼ of pepper. Return bread slices to oven; broil 1 additional minute or until cheese melts. **YIELD:** 4 servings (serving size: 1 toast).

PER SERVING: CAL 99; FAT 2.4g (sat 1g); PRO 5.4g; CARB 12.9g; FIB 0.5g; SUG 0.5g; CHOL 5mg; IRON 0.7mg; SOD 272mg; CALC 101mg

Soup and Salad Menu

PointsPlus **value per serving: 8**

Chili Picante

Tex-Mex Layered Salad

Chili Picante

PointsPlus **value:** 6

PREP: 1 minute ■ **COOK:** 14 minutes

This dish has the flavor and aroma of a chili that has simmered all day—you're the only one who has to know it hasn't. For a crunchy addition, serve this spicy soup and salad combo with baked tortilla chips.

GAME PLAN

❶ While ground beef mixture cooks:

- Rinse and drain beans.
- Measure picante sauce, water, and cumin.

❷ While chili cooks:

- Prepare salad

¾ pound 93% lean ground beef
1 cup refrigerated prechopped tricolor bell pepper
1 cup medium picante sauce
1 cup water
1 (15-ounce) can black beans, rinsed and drained
2 teaspoons ground cumin
½ cup reduced-fat sour cream

1. Heat a large Dutch oven over medium-high heat. Add beef and bell pepper to pan; cook until beef is browned, stirring to crumble beef.
2. Add picante sauce and next 3 ingredients to pan; bring to a boil. Reduce heat, and simmer, uncovered, 8 minutes. Ladle into 4 bowls; top evenly with sour cream. **YIELD:** 4 servings (serving size: about 1 cup chili and 2 tablespoons sour cream).

PER SERVING: CAL 222; FAT 5.6g; (sat 2.7g); PRO 23.5g; CARB 21.7g; FIB 5g; SUG 5.8g; CHOL 55mg; IRON 2.9mg; SOD 498mg; CALC 34mg

Tex-Mex Layered Salad

PointsPlus **value:** 2

PREP: 6 minutes

⅓ cup reduced-fat sour cream
2 tablespoons light mayonnaise
¼ cup bottled chipotle salsa
1 (8-ounce) bag shredded iceberg lettuce
1 cup refrigerated prediced fresh tomato
¼ cup finely chopped red onion
¼ cup (1 ounce) reduced-fat shredded sharp cheddar cheese

1. Combine sour cream, mayonnaise, and salsa in a small bowl. Place lettuce in a large bowl; spoon sour cream mixture over lettuce. Layer tomato, red onion, and cheese over sour cream mixture. Cover and chill until ready to serve. **YIELD:** 4 servings (serving size: 1½ cups).

PER SERVING: CAL 81; FAT 4g; (sat 2g); PRO 3.4g; CARB 9.3g; FIB 1.8g; SUG 5.1g; CHOL 12mg; IRON 0.4mg; SOD 268mg; CALC 67mg

Comfort Food Menu

PointsPlus **value per serving: 11**

Smothered Steak

Homestyle Smashed Potatoes

1 cup steamed broccoli >> ***PointsPlus*** value: 0

Smothered Steak

PointsPlus **value:** 7

PREP: 5 minutes ■ **COOK:** 24 minutes

- 3 tablespoons all-purpose flour
- ¼ teaspoon salt
- ¼ teaspoon freshly ground black pepper
- 4 (4-ounce) cubed steak pieces
- ¾ cup fat-free, lower-sodium beef broth
- 2 teaspoons canola oil
- Cooking spray
- ¾ cup thinly vertically sliced onion (1 small onion)

1. Combine first 3 ingredients. Dredge steak in flour mixture, shaking off excess. Reserve excess flour mixture. Combine reserved flour mixture and broth in a 1-cup glass measure, stirring with a small whisk; set aside.
2. Heat oil in a large nonstick skillet over medium-high heat. Add steak to pan. Cook 3 minutes on each side or until brown. Remove from pan.
3. Coat pan with cooking spray. Add onion to pan; sauté 5 minutes or until tender. Stir in broth mixture, scraping pan to loosen browned bits. Return steak to pan. Bring to a boil; cover, reduce heat, and simmer 7 minutes or until gravy thickens and steak is tender. Serve sauce over steak. **YIELD:** 4 servings (serving size: 3 ounces steak and ¼ cup sauce).

PER SERVING: CAL 291; FAT 13.7g (sat 3.4g); PRO 24.2g; CARB 16.3g; FIB 0.9g; SUG 1.4g; CHOL 64mg; IRON 3.7mg; SOD 394mg; CALC 47mg

GAME PLAN

❶ While steak cooks:
■ Microwave potatoes.

❷ While broccoli steams:
■ Season potatoes.

Homestyle Smashed Potatoes

PointsPlus **value:** 4

PREP: 2 minutes ■ **COOK:** 8 minutes

- 1 pound red potatoes (about 5)
- 1 cup nonfat buttermilk
- ¼ cup grated Parmesan cheese
- 2 tablespoons yogurt-based spread
- ¼ teaspoon salt
- ¼ teaspoon freshly ground black pepper

1. Place potatoes in a single layer in a microwave-safe bowl (do not pierce potatoes with a fork). Cover bowl with plastic wrap (do not allow plastic wrap to touch food); vent. Microwave at HIGH 8 minutes or until tender.
2. Add buttermilk and remaining ingredients to potatoes. Mash potato mixture with a potato masher until creamy. **YIELD:** 4 servings (serving size: about ½ cup).

PER SERVING: CAL 169; FAT 4.8g (sat 2g); PRO 7.9g; CARB 23.6g; FIB 1.4g; SUG 1g; CHOL 8mg; IRON 1mg; SOD 385mg; CALC 166mg

Asian Pork Chop Menu

PointsPlus value per serving: 8

Hoisin-Orange Pork Chops

Coconut Rice

½ cup steamed sugar snap peas >> ***PointsPlus*** value: 0

GAME PLAN

❶ While broiler preheats:
- Prepare hoisin mixture for pork.

❷ While pork cooks:
- Cook rice.

❸ While rice cooks:
- Toast coconut.
- Cook bell pepper.

❹ While peas cook:
- Toss rice with coconut and bell pepper.

Hoisin-Orange Pork Chops

PointsPlus **value:** 5

PREP: 3 minutes ■ **COOK:** 8 minutes

Perk up humble pork chops with a sweet hoisin sauce and aromatic Chinese five-spice powder—a blend of cinnamon, cloves, fennel seed, star anise, and Szechuan peppercorns.

3 tablespoons hoisin sauce
2 teaspoons grated orange rind
1 teaspoon lower-sodium soy sauce
¼ teaspoon five-spice powder
4 (4-ounce) boneless center-cut loin pork chops (½ inch thick)
1 teaspoon dark sesame oil
Cooking spray

1. Preheat broiler.
2. Combine first 4 ingredients in a small bowl; stir with a whisk.
3. Rub pork chops with sesame oil, and baste with hoisin mixture. Place pork on a broiler pan coated with cooking spray, and cook 4 minutes on each side or until done, basting occasionally with remaining hoisin mixture. **YIELD:** 4 servings (serving size: 1 pork chop).

PER SERVING: CAL 198; FAT 8.1g (sat 2.5g); PRO 24.3g; CARB 5.6g; FIB 0.1g; SUG 3.8g; CHOL 65mg; IRON 0.7mg; SOD 279mg; CALC 26mg

Coconut Rice

PointsPlus **value:** 3

PREP: 3 minutes ■ **COOK:** 6 minutes

1 (8.8-ounce) package precooked whole-grain brown rice (such as Uncle Ben's Ready Rice)
¼ cup flaked sweetened coconut
Cooking spray
½ cup diced red bell pepper

1. Microwave rice according to package directions.
2. While rice cooks, heat a small nonstick skillet over medium-high heat. Add coconut to pan; cook 2 minutes or until golden brown, stirring constantly. Remove coconut, and set aside. Return pan to medium-high heat; coat pan with cooking spray. Add bell pepper to pan; cook 2 minutes or until crisp-tender. Combine rice, coconut, and bell pepper in a medium bowl; toss well. **YIELD:** 4 servings (serving size: ½ cup).

PER SERVING: CAL 124; FAT 3.1g (sat 1.5g); PRO 2.6g; CARB 21.8g; FIB 1.7g; SUG 2.4g; CHOL 0mg; IRON 0.5mg; SOD 16mg; CALC 2mg

Company's Coming Menu

PointsPlus **value per serving: 8**

Chicken Cutlets with Fontina and Fresh Blueberry Sauce

Ginger-Roasted Green Beans

1 (1.3-ounce) dinner roll >> ***PointsPlus*** value: 2

Chicken Cutlets with Fontina and Fresh Blueberry Sauce

PointsPlus **value:** 5

PREP: 5 minutes ■ **COOK:** 10 minutes

Buttery fontina cheese and a sweet-savory, jewel-toned blueberry sauce turn modest chicken cutlets into an extraordinary dish that family and friends will love.

- 1 tablespoon butter, divided
- ¾ pound chicken cutlets (about 4 cutlets)
- ½ teaspoon salt
- ¼ teaspoon freshly ground black pepper
- ½ cup (2 ounces) shredded fontina cheese
- 3 tablespoons apple juice
- 1 tablespoon rice wine vinegar
- ½ teaspoon Dijon mustard
- 1 cup fresh blueberries
- 1½ teaspoons minced fresh thyme

1. Melt 1 teaspoon butter in a large nonstick skillet over medium-high heat. Sprinkle chicken with salt and pepper. Add chicken to pan; cook 3 minutes on each side or until done. Remove chicken to a serving platter; sprinkle with cheese. Keep warm.

2. Combine apple juice, vinegar, and mustard in a small bowl; stir well with a whisk. Add apple juice mixture to pan; simmer 1 minute. Add blueberries and thyme; simmer 2 minutes. Stir in remaining 2 teaspoons butter. Spoon blueberry sauce over chicken. **YIELD:** 4 servings (serving size: about 1 chicken cutlet and 2 tablespoons sauce).

PER SERVING: CAL 199; FAT 8.2g (sat 4.7g); PRO 23.4g; CARB 7.2g; FIB 1g; SUG 5.2g; CHOL 73mg; IRON 0.8mg; SOD 491mg; CALC 89mg

GAME PLAN

❶ While oven preheats:

- Grate ginger, mince thyme, and shred cheese.

❷ While green beans cook:

- Cook chicken.
- Cook blueberry sauce.
- Warm dinner rolls.

Ginger-Roasted Green Beans

PointsPlus **value:** 1

PREP: 2 minutes ■ **COOK:** 10 minutes

- 1 (12-ounce) package pretrimmed green beans
- 2 teaspoons olive oil
- 2 teaspoons grated peeled fresh ginger
- ⅛ teaspoon salt

1. Preheat oven to 450°.

2. Combine green beans, olive oil, ginger, and salt on a rimmed baking sheet; toss well. Spread beans in a single layer. Bake at 450° for 10 minutes or until crisp-tender. **YIELD:** 4 servings (serving size: about ¾ cup).

PER SERVING: CAL 47; FAT 2.4g (sat 0.4g); PRO 1.6g; CARB 62g; FIB 2.9g; SUG 1.2g; CHOL 0mg; IRON 0.9mg; SOD 78mg; CALC 32mg

Dinner for Two Menu

PointsPlus **value per serving: 5**

Dilled Salmon Cakes with Tzatziki Sauce

Cucumber and Cherry Tomato Salad

Dilled Salmon Cakes with Tzatziki Sauce

PointsPlus **value:** 4

PREP: 7 minutes ■ **COOK:** 7 minutes

Tzatziki is a traditional Greek sauce made with yogurt, cucumbers, and lemon. Its tangy flavor pairs perfectly with the warm, tender salmon cakes.

GAME PLAN

❶ Prepare vegetables for salmon patties and salad.

❷ Chop dill, and prepare patties.

❸ While patties cook:

- Prepare cucumber sauce.
- Prepare salad.

- 2 (6-ounce) cans skinless, boneless pink salmon in water, drained (such as Bumble Bee)
- ⅓ cup dry breadcrumbs
- 3 tablespoons chopped green onions
- 1 tablespoon chopped fresh dill
- 1 large egg
- ⅛ teaspoon freshly ground black pepper
- 2 teaspoons canola oil
- ¼ cup plain low-fat yogurt
- ¼ cup grated seeded peeled cucumber
- ½ teaspoon grated lemon rind
- ⅛ teaspoon salt

1. Combine first 6 ingredients in a medium bowl. Shape mixture into 4 (½-inch-thick) patties.

2. Heat oil in a large nonskillet over medium-high heat. Add salmon patties to pan; cook 3 to 4 minutes on each side or until browned.

3. While patties cook, combine yogurt and remaining ingredients. To serve, spoon cucumber sauce over salmon cakes. **YIELD:** 2 servings (serving size: 2 salmon cakes and about ¼ cup sauce).

PER SERVING: CAL 188; FAT 7.4g (sat 1.3g); PRO 20.6g; CARB 29.3g; FIB 5.7g; SUG 4g; CHOL 76mg; IRON 3.5mg; SOD 562mg; CALC 306mg

Cucumber and Cherry Tomato Salad with Balsamic Vinaigrette

PointsPlus **value:** 1

PREP: 5 minutes

- ½ pint cherry tomatoes, halved
- 1 cup sliced cucumber
- ¼ cup halved and thinly sliced sweet onion
- 1 tablespoon balsamic vinegar
- ½ teaspoon sugar
- ½ teaspoon extra-virgin olive oil
- ⅛ teaspoon salt
- ⅛ teaspoon freshly ground black pepper

1. Combine tomato, cucumber, and onion in a medium bowl. Combine vinegar, sugar, olive oil, salt, and pepper in a small bowl; stir with a whisk. Pour dressing over salad; toss well. **YIELD:** 2 servings (serving size: about 1 cup).

PER SERVING: CAL 50; FAT 1.5g (sat 0.2g); PRO 1.2g; CARB 8.7g; FIB 1.5g; SUG 3.9g; CHOL 0mg; IRON 0.6mg; SOD 156mg; CALC 17mg

appetizers, snacks & beverages

Try these no-fuss recipes when you need tasty party starters, satisfying bites, and refreshing drinks.

Kalamata-and-Herbed Cheese Mini Phyllos

***PointsPlus* value:** 3
PREP: 16 minutes

Tangy Greek kalamata olives and creamy herb-flavored cheese make an irresistible filling for prepared phyllo shells. Topped with fresh basil and tomatoes, these pretty mini appetizers received one of our Test Kitchens' highest ratings.

- 15 pitted kalamata olives, divided
- 1/3 cup light garlic-and-herbs spreadable cheese (such as Alouette light)
- 1 (2.1-ounce) package mini phyllo shells (such as Athens)
- 3 tablespoons chopped fresh basil
- 6 grape tomatoes, finely chopped

1. Cut 4 olives lengthwise into 4 wedges each; reserve 15 wedges. Finely chop remaining olive wedge and remaining 11 olives.
2. Combine chopped olives and cheese, stirring well. Spoon about 1 rounded teaspoon of cheese mixture into each phyllo shell.
3. Top cheese mixture evenly with basil and tomato. Garnish stuffed shells with reserved olive wedges. **YIELD:** 5 servings (serving size: 3 appetizers).

PER SERVING: CAL 115; FAT 8.2g (sat 2g); PRO 1.5g; CARB 8.6g; FIB 0.4g; SUG 0g; CHOL 11mg; IRON 0.8mg; SOD 286mg; CALC 18mg

Cheesy Artichoke Crostini

***PointsPlus* value:** 2

PREP: 3 minutes ■ **COOK:** 11 minutes

To save time, place the bread slices in the oven while it preheats. Look for a baguette that is about 3 inches in diameter.

24 (½-inch-thick) slices diagonally cut French bread baguette
Olive oil–flavored cooking spray
2 large garlic cloves
1 (14-ounce) can artichoke hearts, rinsed and drained
¼ cup fresh basil leaves
1 tablespoon extra-virgin olive oil
1 teaspoon grated lemon rind
¼ teaspoon salt
¼ teaspoon freshly ground black pepper
1 plum tomato, quartered
¼ cup (1 ounce) freshly grated Parmigiano-Reggiano cheese

1. Preheat oven to 450°.
2. While oven preheats, place baguette slices on a large baking sheet; coat slices with cooking spray. Place in oven; bake 8 minutes while oven preheats.
3. While bread toasts, drop garlic through food chute of a food processor with processor on; process until minced. Add artichoke and next 6 ingredients; pulse 3 times or until coarsely chopped. Spoon about 1 tablespoon artichoke mixture onto each bread slice. Sprinkle evenly with cheese.
4. Bake crostini at 450° for 3 minutes or until cheese melts. **YIELD:** 12 servings (serving size: 2 crostini).

PER SERVING: CAL 77; FAT 2.2g (sat 0.6g); PRO 3.5g; CARB 11g; FIB 0.5g; SUG 0.6g; CHOL 2mg; IRON 0.9mg; SOD 249mg; CALC 43mg

Smoked Salmon-Wrapped Stuffed Olives

***PointsPlus* value:** 1

PREP: 20 minutes

Ideal for cocktail parties, these no-cook olives are filled with dill-laced cream cheese and wrapped with rich-flavored smoked salmon.

⅓ cup (2½ ounces) tub-style light cream cheese, softened
2 teaspoons chopped fresh dill
¼ teaspoon freshly ground black pepper
14 super colossal–sized pitted ripe olives (such as Lindsay)
2 ounces sliced smoked salmon
14 decorative cocktail picks

1. Combine first 3 ingredients in a small bowl, stirring until smooth. Spoon cheese mixture into a heavy-duty zip-top plastic bag. Seal bag, removing as much air as possible. Snip a small hole in 1 corner of bag; squeeze filling evenly into olives.
2. Cut salmon slices into 3¼ x ½-inch strips. Wrap each olive with a salmon strip; secure with a cocktail pick. **YIELD:** 14 servings (serving size: 1 stuffed olive).

PER SERVING: CAL 30; FAT 2.2g (sat 0.8g); PRO 1.5g; CARB 1.3g; FIB 0.4g; SUG 0.4g; CHOL 4mg; IRON 0.5mg; SOD 195mg; CALC 22mg

Strawberry-Pear Pickled Ginger Salsa

***PointsPlus* value:** 1

PREP: 15 minutes

This colorful salsa pairs nicely with gingersnaps or cinnamon-sugar pita chips, and it also livens up grilled chicken, fish, or pork.

1½ cups finely chopped strawberries
1 cup finely chopped peeled pear (about 1 medium)
1 tablespoon "measures-like-sugar" calorie-free sweetener (such as Splenda)
3 tablespoons finely chopped red onion
2 tablespoons finely chopped pickled ginger
1½ teaspoons grated orange rind

1. Combine all ingredients in a medium bowl. Serve immediately. **YIELD:** 10 servings (serving size: 2 tablespoons).

PER SERVING: CAL 23; FAT 0.1g (sat 0g); PRO 0.3g; CARB 5.6g; FIB 1.2g; SUG 3.4g; CHOL 0mg; IRON 0.2mg; SOD 21mg; CALC 8mg

Strawberry-Pear
Pickled Ginger Salsa

Roasted Red Pepper and Sun-Dried Tomato Dip

Roasted Red Pepper and Sun-Dried Tomato Dip

***PointsPlus* value:** 1
PREP: 8 minutes

Pat the sun-dried tomatoes well with paper towels to remove excess oil before chopping. Serve this creamy dip with toasted bread slices or raw vegetables.

1 cup bottled roasted red bell peppers
1 cup chopped drained oil-packed sun-dried tomatoes
1 (8-ounce) block fat-free cream cheese
⅓ cup (1¼ ounces) crumbled feta cheese
2 tablespoons light mayonnaise
1 tablespoon chopped fresh parsley
2 garlic cloves, halved
½ teaspoon freshly ground black pepper
¼ teaspoon salt

1. Place all ingredients in a blender or food processor; process until blended and desired consistency. Refrigerate, covered, until ready to serve. **YIELD:** 17 servings (serving size: 2 tablespoons).

PER SERVING: CAL 39; FAT 2g (sat 0.7g); PRO 2.7g; CARB 3.2g; FIB 0.4g; SUG 0.5g; CHOL 4mg; IRON 0.2mg; SOD 206mg; CALC 43mg

Masala Pumpkin Seeds

***PointsPlus* value:** 2
PREP: 1 minute ■ **COOK:** 5 minutes

This snack is made in a skillet using an Indian spice blend similar to curry powder called garam masala. The seeds double as a spicy garnish for simple salads or soups.

½ teaspoon canola oil
1 cup raw pumpkin seeds (such as Woodstock Farms)
¾ teaspoon salt-free garam masala (such as Frontier)
¼ teaspoon kosher salt
¼ teaspoon ground cumin
Dash of ground red pepper

1. Heat a cast-iron skillet over medium heat until hot; add oil. Stir in pumpkin seeds.
2. Cook 4 minutes or until seeds are golden and begin to pop, stirring frequently. Cook, stirring constantly, 1 to 2 minutes or until most of the seeds are lightly browned. Remove from heat; stir in garam masala and remaining ingredients. **YIELD:** 16 servings (serving size: 1 tablespoon).

PER SERVING: CAL 65; FAT 5.5g (sat 0.9g); PRO 2.7g; CARB 1.4g; FIB 0.4g; SUG 0g; CHOL 0mg; IRON 0.9mg; SOD 31mg; CALC 1mg

Garam Masala

Garam masala is a popular Indian spice blend that literally means "hot spice." Instead of being "hot" like chiles, this blend deepens the overall flavor profile of meats and vegetables. Unlike most spices, garam masala is usually added at the end of cooking to maintain its rich aroma. Store any unused garam masala in an airtight container in the freezer for up to 6 months.

Italian Crisps

***PointsPlus* value:** 1
PREP: 7 minutes ■ **COOK:** 9 minutes

This crunchy appetizer comes together in minutes and is simple enough to assemble while friends gather in the kitchen.

12 wonton wrappers
Cooking spray
¼ cup commercial pesto
2 plum tomatoes, diced
⅓ cup (1¼ ounces) grated fresh Parmesan cheese

1. Preheat oven to 400°.
2. Cut wonton wrappers in half diagonally to form triangles. Place in a single layer on a baking sheet coated with cooking spray. Spray triangles with cooking spray. Bake at 400° for 6 minutes or until lightly browned.
3. Brush pesto evenly over crisps. Top evenly with tomato and cheese. Bake an additional 3 minutes or until cheese melts. Serve immediately. **YIELD:** 24 servings (serving size: 1 crisp).

PER SERVING: CAL 32; FAT 1.7g (sat 0.4g); PRO 1.4g; CARB 2.8g; FIB 0.2g; SUG 0.3g; CHOL 2mg; IRON 0.2mg; SOD 74mg; CALC 31mg

PB and Honey Dip

***PointsPlus* value:** 2
PREP: 5 minutes

Silken tofu is the secret ingredient that adds creaminess and soy protein to this tasty dip. Serve with apple wedges or as a spread for bagels or toast.

½ cup natural-style creamy peanut butter (such as Smucker's)
½ cup silken tofu (about 4½ ounces)
3 tablespoons honey
1 tablespoon fresh lime juice
⅛ teaspoon ground cinnamon

1. Place all ingredients in a blender or food processor; process until smooth. Refrigerate in an airtight container up to 1 week. **YIELD:** 16 servings (serving size: 1 tablespoon).

PER SERVING: CAL 70; FAT 4.2g (sat 0.7g); PRO 2.6g; CARB 5.1g; FIB 0.5g; SUG 3.6g; CHOL 0mg; IRON 0.1mg; SOD 33mg; CALC 3mg

Natural Peanut Butter

Natural peanut butter has a layer of oil on top that needs to be stirred back into the peanut butter before using. Although not as creamy as regular peanut butter, natural peanut butter is a healthier option because it doesn't contain trans fat, and it's high in monounsaturated fat.

Pumpkin Parmesan Hummus

***PointsPlus* value:** 2
PREP: 13 minutes

This highly rated recipe showcases versatile pumpkin (actually a squash) in a savory role. Serve it with pita chips, red bell pepper, or jicama strips.

2 large garlic cloves
1 (16-ounce) can reduced-sodium garbanzo beans (such as Bush's), rinsed and drained
1 cup canned pumpkin
½ cup (2 ounces) freshly shredded Parmigiano-Reggiano cheese
3 tablespoons fresh lime juice
3 tablespoons plain fat-free Greek yogurt (such as Fage)
1 teaspoon Southwest chipotle seasoning blend (such as Mrs. Dash)
¼ teaspoon salt

1. Drop garlic through food chute of a food processor with processor on. Process until minced. Add garbanzo beans; process until chopped. Add pumpkin and remaining ingredients; process until smooth. **YIELD:** 10 servings (serving size: ¼ cup).

PER SERVING: CAL 62; FAT 2.1g (sat 0.8g); PRO 4.8g; CARB 7.4g; FIB 1.8g; SUG 1.2g; CHOL 4mg; IRON 0.4mg; SOD 272mg; CALC 99mg

Hot Spiced Chocolate

***PointsPlus* value:** 4

PREP: 4 minutes ■ **COOK:** 17 minutes

Ginger flavor comes through in this warm chocolate treat. You can use fat-free milk if that's what you have on hand.

4 cups 1% low-fat milk
3 tablespoons chopped crystallized ginger
8 whole cloves
2 (3-inch) cinnamon sticks, broken in half
⅓ cup fat-free chocolate syrup (such as Hershey's)

1. Combine first 4 ingredients in a medium saucepan. Bring to a boil; reduce heat, and simmer 12 minutes. Remove from heat.

2. Strain milk mixture through a sieve over a bowl, discarding spices. Return milk to saucepan. Stir in chocolate syrup. Cook over low heat just until thoroughly heated. Serve hot. **YIELD:** 6 servings (serving size: about ¾ cup).

PER SERVING: CAL 159; FAT 1.7g (sat 1.1g); PRO 6.1g; CARB 29.5g; FIB 0.7g; SUG 26g; CHOL 7mg; IRON 0.1mg; SOD 96mg; CALC 200mg

Crystallized Ginger

Crystallized ginger is generally found in supermarket spice sections or in produce departments' specialty areas. Before chopping crystallized ginger, coat your knife with cooking spray to keep the ginger from sticking to it.

Pomegranate Refreshers

Pomegranate Refreshers

***PointsPlus* value:** 2
PREP: 4 minutes

Pomegranate and lemon juices mingle to make this antioxidant-packed beverage a real crowd pleaser.

2 cups pomegranate juice, chilled
¼ cup fresh lemon juice
3 tablespoons sugar
2 cups club soda, chilled
Ice cubes
Lemon slices (optional)

1. Combine first 3 ingredients in a small pitcher, stirring until sugar dissolves. Gently stir in club soda. Serve over ice, and garnish with lemon slices, if desired. **YIELD:** 6 servings (serving size: about ¾ cup).

PER SERVING: CAL 73; FAT 0g; PRO 0.4g; CARB 18.8g; FIB 0g; SUG 17.8g; CHOL 0mg; IRON 0.1mg; SOD 27mg; CALC 18mg

Citrus Green Tea-Mint Sparkler

***PointsPlus* value:** 0
PREP: 3 minutes

Gently crushing the fresh mint leaves in the glass releases the herb's wonderful aromatic oils. Our recipe is for 1 generous serving, but multiplying the ingredients and serving in a pitcher also works well.

3 large fresh mint leaves
1 cup crushed ice
1 cup sugar-free citrus green tea (such as Lipton), chilled
⅓ cup diet citrus soda (such as original Fresca), chilled
1 lime wedge

1. Place mint leaves in a tall glass; press leaves with the end of a wooden spoon several times. Add crushed ice to glass. Pour green tea and soda over ice; squeeze lime juice into glass. Stir well before serving. **YIELD:** 1 serving (serving size: 1¾ cups).

PER SERVING: CAL 1.4; FAT 0g; PRO 0g; CARB 0.4g; FIB 0g; SUG 0.1g; CHOL 0mg; IRON 0mg; SOD 72mg; CALC 1.1mg

Whiskey Sour Punch

***PointsPlus* value:** 7
PREP: 7 minutes

We think you will love this version of the classic cocktail as much as everyone in our Test Kitchens did. Sparkling water extends the volume and flavor without adding a single calorie.

1½ cups bourbon
½ (12-ounce) can frozen lemonade concentrate, thawed and undiluted (about ¾ cup)
Ice cubes
2 cups sparkling water
6 red maraschino cherries
6 thin lemon slices

1. Combine bourbon and lemonade concentrate in a pitcher, stirring until concentrate dissolves.
2. Fill 6 tall glasses with ice. Pour ⅓ cup bourbon mixture and ⅓ cup sparkling water into each glass; stir gently. Place 1 cherry and 1 lemon slice in each glass. Serve immediately. **YIELD:** 6 servings (serving size: ⅔ cup).

PER SERVING: CAL 203; FAT 0.1g; PRO 0.1g; CARB 19.4g; FIB 0.2g; SUG 18.1g; CHOL 0mg; IRON 0.3mg; SOD 2mg; CALC 5mg

main dishes

Perfect for family meals and for entertaining guests, these simple but flavorfully prepared entrées offer an array of dinner options no matter what the occasion.

Greek-Style Shrimp Sauté

***PointsPlus* value:** 5

PREP: 2 minutes ■ **COOK:** 6 minutes

An authentic Greek trio of tomatoes, olives, and feta cheese accompanies this shrimp dish. Serve over orzo, and garnish with lemon wedges, if desired.

Cooking spray
4 tablespoons light olive oil vinaigrette, divided (such as Ken's Steak House Lite)
1½ pounds peeled and deveined large shrimp
1 cup grape tomatoes, halved
12 chopped pitted kalamata olives
¼ cup chopped fresh basil
⅓ cup (1.3 ounces) crumbled reduced-fat feta cheese
Chopped fresh basil (optional)
Lemon wedges (optional)

1. Heat a large nonstick skillet over medium-high heat. Coat pan with cooking spray. Add 1 tablespoon vinaigrette and shrimp. Cook shrimp 3 minutes or until done, stirring frequently.

2. Remove shrimp from pan; keep warm. Add tomato, 3 tablespoons vinaigrette, olives, and basil to pan. Cook 1 minute or until tomato is thoroughly heated. Remove pan from heat. Return shrimp to pan; toss gently. Sprinkle with cheese and additional basil, if desired; toss well. Serve with lemon wedges, if desired. **YIELD:** 4 servings (serving size: 1 cup).

PER SERVING: CAL 219; FAT 8.8g (sat 1.9g); PRO 29.8g; CARB 4.5g; FIB 0.9g; SUG 1g; CHOL 255mg; IRON 4.2mg; SOD 742mg; CALC 89mg

Seared Scallops with Soy-Ginger Sauce

***PointsPlus* value:** 4

PREP: 4 minutes ■ **COOK:** 6 minutes

This super-fast entrée features succulent sea scallops and is perfect for an intimate gathering, since it comes together so quickly. To ensure crisp, browned scallops, pat any excess moisture from them just before seasoning and pan searing. Serve with a side of carrots.

3 tablespoons lower-sodium soy sauce
2 tablespoons chopped green onions
1 tablespoon honey
1 tablespoon chopped peeled fresh ginger
⅛ teaspoon crushed red pepper
1½ pounds large sea scallops (12 scallops)
¼ teaspoon kosher salt
¼ teaspoon freshly ground black pepper
Cooking spray
Thinly sliced green onions (optional)

1. Combine soy sauce and next 4 ingredients in a bowl.

2. Pat scallops dry with paper towels, and sprinkle with salt and pepper. Heat a large nonstick skillet over medium-high heat. Coat pan with cooking spray. Add scallops to pan, and cook 3 minutes on each side until browned. Transfer scallops to a platter; drizzle with soy sauce mixture. Garnish with sliced green onions, if desired. **YIELD:** 4 servings (serving size: 3 scallops and about 1¼ teaspoons sauce).

PER SERVING: CAL 175; FAT 1.3g (sat 0.1g); PRO 29.3g; CARB 10g; FIB 0.3g; SUG 4.5g; CHOL 56mg; IRON 0.8mg; SOD 792mg; CALC 46mg

Poached Salmon with Lemon-Caper Sauce

***PointsPlus* value:** 7

PREP: 3 minutes ■ **COOK:** 12 minutes

When poaching salmon, have the cooking liquid at a bare simmer because it requires gentle heat. Serve this buttery entrée with a mound of polenta topped with a fresh tomato sauce.

4 (6-ounce) salmon fillets, skinned
⅛ teaspoon salt
3 fresh parsley sprigs
2 fresh oregano sprigs
⅓ cup dry white wine
3 tablespoons drained capers
1 tablespoon light butter
2 teaspoons fresh lemon juice

1. Sprinkle fish with salt; place in a large skillet. Add parsley and oregano sprigs and wine. Fill pan with enough water to come halfway up sides of fish. Bring to a boil; reduce heat, and simmer 4 minutes. Turn fish over, and simmer 3 to 4 minutes or until fish flakes easily when tested with a fork. Remove and discard herbs. Transfer fish to a serving platter; keep warm.
2. Add capers to cooking liquid. Bring to a boil; boil 2 minutes or until liquid is reduced to 3 tablespoons. Whisk in butter and lemon juice. Serve over fish. **YIELD:** 4 servings (serving size: 1 fillet and about 1 tablespoon sauce).

PER SERVING: CAL 267; FAT 11.4g (sat 2.7g); PRO 38.7g; CARB 3.2g; FIB 0.4g; SUG 0.1g; CHOL 102mg; IRON 1.3mg; SOD 379mg; CALC 19mg

Bay-Scented Snapper with Lemon

***PointsPlus* value:** 5

PREP: 6 minutes ■ **COOK:** 9 minutes

The seasoning combination of lemon and bay leaves makes versatile snapper simply delicious. Substitute tilapia or flounder for the snapper, if desired.

1 teaspoon grated lemon rind
1 tablespoon olive oil
4 (6-ounce) red snapper fillets
¼ teaspoon salt
¼ teaspoon freshly ground black pepper
Cooking spray
8 fresh bay leaves
8 lemon slices
4 lemon wedges

1. Preheat broiler.
2. Combine lemon rind and oil in a small bowl; set aside.
3. Sprinkle fillets with salt and pepper. Place fish on a broiler pan coated with cooking spray. Drizzle lemon mixture over fish. Arrange 2 bay leaves on each fillet. Top with 2 lemon slices. Broil 9 to 10 minutes or until fish flakes easily when tested with a fork. Serve with lemon wedges. **YIELD:** 4 servings (serving size: 1 fillet).

PER SERVING: CAL 205; FAT 5.8g (sat 1g); PRO 35.1g; CARB 1.5g; FIB 0.5g; SUG 0.4g; CHOL 63mg; IRON 0.4mg; SOD 255mg; CALC 59mg

Spicy Fish Sticks with Chipotle Ketchup

PointsPlus **value:** 7

PREP: 7 minutes ■ **COOK:** 4 minutes

Adding a few full-flavored ingredients takes this family favorite from routine to robust. Look for chipotle chile powder and salt-free Cajun seasoning alongside dried herbs and spices in the supermarket.

½ cup ketchup
¼ teaspoon chipotle chile powder
¼ cup plain yellow cornmeal
3 tablespoons all-purpose flour
1½ teaspoons salt-free Cajun seasoning
1½ teaspoons dried parsley
½ teaspoon garlic salt, divided
4 (6-ounce) mahimahi or other firm white fish fillets
2 tablespoons canola oil

1. Combine ketchup and chipotle chile powder in a small bowl. Set aside.
2. Combine cornmeal, flour, Cajun seasoning, parsley, and ¼ teaspoon garlic salt in a shallow dish. Cut each fillet in half lengthwise, then in half crosswise. Press fish between paper towels until barely moist; sprinkle with remaining ¼ teaspoon garlic salt, and dredge in cornmeal mixture.
3. Heat oil in a large nonstick skillet over medium-high heat. Add fish; cook 2 minutes on each side or until fish flakes easily when tested with a fork. Serve with ketchup mixture. **YIELD:** 4 servings (serving size: 4 fish sticks and 2 tablespoons ketchup mixture).

PER SERVING: CAL 265; FAT 8.3g (sat 0.8g); PRO 32.7g; CARB 13.8g; FIB 0.3g; SUG 6.9g; CHOL 124mg; IRON 2.4mg; SOD 610mg; CALC 32mg

Chipotle Chile Powder

Don't confuse this smoky, sweet spice with regular chili powder. The latter is a general combination of ground chile peppers and various spices like garlic powder, oregano, and cumin, while the former is quite specific—a pure product of ground dried jalapeño chiles. It contributes a spicy heat to sauces, grilling rubs, and chilis.

Taco Seasoned Sirloin with Fresh Tomatoes

PointsPlus **value:** 4

PREP: 5 minutes ■ **COOK:** 12 minutes ■ **OTHER:** 3 minutes

Zippy taco seasoning and fresh lime juice enhance the flavor of this quick sirloin steak main dish.

1 pound boneless sirloin steak
2 tablespoons less-sodium taco seasoning
Cooking spray
1 cup grape tomatoes, halved
6 tablespoons water
2 teaspoons olive oil
1 large lime

1. Coat both sides of steak evenly with taco seasoning.
2. Heat a large nonstick skillet over medium-high heat. Coat pan with cooking spray. Cook steak 4 minutes on each side or until desired degree of doneness. Let stand 3 minutes. Cut steak diagonally across grain into thin slices. Set aside, and keep warm.
3. Recoat pan with cooking spray. Add grape tomatoes and 6 tablespoons water; cook 3 minutes or until tomatoes are soft, scraping pan to loosen browned bits. Remove from heat; stir in oil.
4. Cut lime in half lengthwise. Cut 1 half into 4 wedges. Squeeze remaining lime half evenly over steak slices. Serve steak slices with tomato mixture and lime wedges. **YIELD:** 4 servings (serving size: 3 ounces steak and 2 tablespoons tomato mixture).

PER SERVING: CAL 179; FAT 6.9g (sat 2g); PRO 22.7g; CARB 5.4g; FIB 0.5g; SUG 1.2g; CHOL 42mg; IRON 1.6mg; SOD 347mg; CALC 18mg

Beef Tenderloin Steaks with Red Wine-Mushroom Sauce

***PointsPlus* value:** 6

PREP: 1 minute ■ **COOK:** 10 minutes

Stirring the mushrooms constantly helps release their juices, allowing them to caramelize quickly.

- 4 (4-ounce) beef tenderloin steaks, trimmed (about ½ inch thick)
- ¼ teaspoon salt
- ¼ teaspoon freshly ground black pepper
- Butter-flavored cooking spray
- 1 (8-ounce) package presliced baby portobello mushrooms
- 1 cup dry red wine
- 2 tablespoons butter
- 1 teaspoon minced fresh rosemary

1. Heat a large nonstick skillet over medium-high heat. Sprinkle steaks with salt and pepper; coat with cooking spray. Add steaks to pan; cook 3 minutes on each side or until desired degree of doneness. Transfer steaks to a serving platter; keep warm.

2. Add mushrooms to pan. Coat mushrooms with cooking spray; sauté 3 minutes or until browned. Stir in wine, scraping pan to loosen browned bits. Cook until liquid almost evaporates. Remove pan from heat; add butter and rosemary, stirring until butter melts. Pour sauce over steaks. **YIELD:** 4 servings (serving size: 1 steak and ¼ cup sauce).

PER SERVING: CAL 269; FAT 12.5g (sat 6g); PRO 23.3g; CARB 4.5g; FIB 0.9g; SUG 1.4g; CHOL 74mg; IRON 1.9mg; SOD 235mg; CALC 24mg

Pork Tenderloin with Balsamic Onion-Fig Relish

PointsPlus **value:** 6

PREP: 4 minutes ■ **COOK:** 20 minutes ■ **OTHER:** 5 minutes

- 1 (1-pound) pork tenderloin, trimmed
- ¼ teaspoon salt
- ¼ teaspoon freshly ground black pepper
- Cooking spray
- 8 dried Mission figs
- 2 tablespoons balsamic vinegar
- 2 tablespoons water
- 1 tablespoon lower-sodium soy sauce
- 1 (8-ounce) container refrigerated prechopped onion

1. Preheat oven to 425°.

2. Sprinkle pork evenly with salt and pepper; coat with cooking spray. Heat a medium-sized cast-iron skillet or other ovenproof skillet over medium-high heat. Coat pan with cooking spray. Add pork; cook 4 minutes or until browned on all sides, turning occasionally.

3. While pork browns, coarsely chop figs. Combine vinegar, 2 tablespoons water, and soy sauce in a small bowl. When pork is browned, remove pan from heat. Add figs, onion, and vinegar mixture to pan, stirring to loosen browned bits.

4. Bake, uncovered, at 425° for 15 minutes or until a thermometer registers 160° (slightly pink). Stir onion mixture; cover pan loosely with foil. Let stand 5 minutes before slicing. **YIELD:** 4 servings (serving size: 3 ounces pork and ¼ cup relish).

PER SERVING: CAL 256; FAT 4g (sat 1.4g); PRO 24.6g; CARB 30.6g; FIB 4.6g; SUG 21.5g; CHOL 63mg; IRON 2.1mg; SOD 349mg; CALC 81mg

Bare Burrito

***PointsPlus* value:** 9
PREP: 5 minutes ■ **COOK:** 10 minutes

Precooked rice, preshredded cheese, and preshredded lettuce are all great time-savers.

1 pound ground sirloin
½ cup chopped onion
½ cup chopped green bell pepper
1 (8¾-ounce) can no-salt-added whole-kernel corn, drained
1 (4.4-ounce) package precooked brown rice (such as Minute ready-to-serve)
1 cup bottled salsa
½ teaspoon coarsely ground black pepper
4 cups shredded iceberg lettuce
¼ cup (1 ounce) reduced-fat shredded cheddar cheese
¼ cup reduced-fat sour cream

1. Cook first 3 ingredients in a large nonstick skillet over medium-high heat until beef is browned, stirring to crumble. (Drain if necessary, and return to pan.) Stir in corn and next 3 ingredients. Cook 2 minutes or until thoroughly heated, stirring frequently.
2. Divide lettuce evenly among plates. Top with beef mixture, cheese, and sour cream. **YIELD:** 4 servings (serving size: 1 cup lettuce, 1 cup beef mixture, 1 tablespoon cheese, and 1 tablespoon sour cream).

PER SERVING: CAL 362; FAT 15.6g (sat 6.8g); PRO 29.2g; CARB 26g; FIB 3.5g; SUG 7.3g; CHOL 86mg; IRON 3.3mg; SOD 541mg; CALC 123mg

Beef and Pepperoni Pizza

***PointsPlus* value:** 9
PREP: 2 minutes ■ **COOK:** 13 minutes

We've reduced the fat, calories, and sodium in a pizzeria-style meat pizza by 50% without sacrificing the delicious and satisfying taste.

1 (10-ounce) Italian whole-wheat thin pizza crust (such as Boboli)
½ pound extra lean ground beef
1 (8-ounce) package sliced fresh mushrooms
Olive oil–flavored cooking spray
¾ cup marinara sauce (such as Newman's Own)
¼ cup turkey pepperoni (about 15 slices)
⅔ cup shredded part-skim mozzarella cheese
¼ teaspoon crushed red pepper

1. Preheat oven to 450°.
2. Place pizza crust on rack in oven while preheating, and heat 5 minutes.
3. While crust heats, sauté beef and mushrooms in a large nonstick skillet coated with cooking spray over medium-high heat 5 minutes or until beef is browned; drain.
4. Remove crust from oven; place on an ungreased baking sheet. Coat crust with cooking spray; spread marinara sauce over crust, leaving a 1-inch border. Top with beef mixture, pepperoni, and cheese. Sprinkle evenly with red pepper.
5. Bake at 450° for 7 to 10 minutes or until crust is golden and cheese is melted. Cut into 8 wedges. Serve immediately. **YIELD:** 4 servings (serving size: 2 slices).

PER SERVING: CAL 367; FAT 11.5g (sat 5.3g); PRO 29.1g; CARB 7.4g; FIB 6.8g; SUG 1.1g; CHOL 49mg; IRON 2.8mg; SOD 810mg; CALC 216mg

Pork Chops with Pomegranate-Orange Reduction

PointsPlus **value:** 5

PREP: 4 minutes ■ **COOK:** 10 minutes

You can find pomegranate juice blends in the refrigerated section of the grocery store alongside the orange juice.

½ teaspoon chili powder
¼ teaspoon ground allspice
¼ teaspoon ground red pepper
¼ teaspoon salt
4 (4-ounce) boneless center-cut loin pork chops (½ inch thick)
Cooking spray
½ cup blueberry-pomegranate juice
2 tablespoons balsamic vinegar
1 tablespoon sugar
1 teaspoon grated orange rind

1. Combine first 4 ingredients in a small bowl, and sprinkle over both sides of pork.
2. Heat a large nonstick skillet over medium-high heat. Coat pan with cooking spray. Add pork chops, and cook 3 to 4 minutes on each side or until done. Remove chops from pan; keep warm.
3. Add blueberry-pomegranate juice, vinegar, and sugar to pan; bring to a boil over medium heat. Cook 3 minutes or until mixture is slightly syrupy. Remove pan from heat, and stir in orange rind. Drizzle sauce evenly over pork chops. **YIELD:** 4 servings (serving size: 1 chop and about 2 teaspoons sauce).

PER SERVING: CAL 198; FAT 6.4g (sat 2.3g); PRO 24g; CARB 9g; FIB 0.2g; SUG 7.7g; CHOL 65mg; IRON 0.8mg; SOD 207mg; CALC 31mg

Reductions

A reduction is created when juice, wine, vinegar, or other liquids are added to pan drippings from meats or juices from vegetables, then simmered until the volume of liquid is "reduced" to about half. This concentrates the flavors so that very little sauce is needed to give your dish a smooth, flavorful finish.

Lamb Chops with Skordalia

PointsPlus **value:** 8

PREP: 4 minutes ■ **COOK:** 11 minutes

A package of refrigerated mashed potatoes jump-starts this version of skordalia, a Greek sauce that's traditionally made with pureed potatoes.

1 lemon, halved and divided
8 (4-ounce) lamb loin chops, trimmed
2 teaspoons salt-free Greek seasoning
¼ teaspoon salt
¼ teaspoon freshly ground black pepper
¼ cup fat-free, lower-sodium chicken broth
6 garlic cloves, pressed
1 teaspoon olive oil
1 tablespoon water
½ cup fat-free milk
1¼ cups refrigerated mashed potatoes (such as Simply Potatoes)

1. Squeeze half of lemon over both sides of lamb chops. Sprinkle lamb evenly with Greek seasoning, salt, and pepper. Set aside.
2. Bring broth and garlic to a boil over medium-high heat. Reduce heat to low, and simmer 7 minutes or until broth almost evaporates.
3. While broth mixture cooks, heat oil in a large nonstick skillet over medium-high heat. Add lamb chops to pan; cook 3 minutes on each side or until desired degree of doneness. Remove from pan, and keep warm. Add 1 tablespoon water to pan, and cook 30 seconds, stirring to loosen browned bits from bottom of pan. Spoon pan juices over lamb chops.
4. Add milk to broth mixture, and bring to a boil over medium heat. Stir in potatoes until smooth. Cook 1 minute or until thoroughly heated. Spoon potato mixture evenly onto 4 serving plates. Place 2 lamb chops atop potatoes on each plate. Drizzle lamb evenly with accumulated juices. Cut remaining lemon half into 4 wedges, and serve with lamb. **YIELD:** 4 servings (serving size: 2 lamb chops, about ½ cup skordalia, about 1 teaspoon pan juices, and 1 lemon wedge).

PER SERVING: CAL 300; FAT 12.7g (sat 5.1g); PRO 31.2g; CARB 14.3g; FIB 1.1g; SUG 2.6g; CHOL 91mg; IRON 2.2mg; SOD 400mg; CALC 75mg

Apricot-Lemon Chicken

PointsPlus **value:** 6

PREP: 4 minutes ■ **COOK:** 14 minutes

Start with an apricot fruit spread to concoct a sauce that transforms simply prepared chicken breast into this elegant dish. Sweet Lemon-Mint-Pear Salad on page 57 makes a delicious partner to this easy-to-prepare entrée.

1 teaspoon curry powder
½ teaspoon salt
¼ teaspoon freshly ground black pepper
4 (6-ounce) skinless, boneless chicken breast halves
Cooking spray
⅓ cup apricot spread (such as Polaner All Fruit)
2 tablespoons fresh lemon juice
2 tablespoons water
2 teaspoons grated lemon rind

1. Combine first 3 ingredients in a small bowl; rub mixture over chicken.
2. Place a large nonstick skillet over medium-high heat. Coat pan with cooking spray. Cook chicken 6 minutes on each side or until done. Remove chicken from pan, and keep warm.
3. Add apricot spread, lemon juice, and 2 tablespoons water to pan, stirring until smooth. Cook over medium heat 1 minute. Spoon sauce over chicken; sprinkle with lemon rind. **YIELD:** 4 servings (serving size: 1 chicken breast half and about 1½ tablespoons apricot-lemon sauce).

PER SERVING: CAL 245; FAT 2g (sat 0.6g); PRO 39.4g; CARB 14.5g; FIB 0.3g; SUG 10.9g; CHOL 99mg; IRON 1.4mg; SOD 402mg; CALC 24mg

Chicken and Shiitake Marsala

Chicken and Shiitake Marsala

***PointsPlus* value:** 6

PREP: 1 minute ■ **COOK:** 14 minutes

Marsala, a fortified Italian wine recognized for its golden brown color and sweet, nutty flavor, is used in both sweet and savory dishes. Along with the smoky mushrooms in this recipe, this wine creates a rich, aromatic sauce. Dry sherry is a good substitute for the Marsala.

4 (6-ounce) skinless, boneless chicken breast halves
Cooking spray
¼ teaspoon salt
¼ teaspoon pepper
2 (3½-ounce) packages shiitake mushrooms, sliced
½ cup Marsala wine
2 green onions, finely chopped (about ⅓ cup) and divided
2 tablespoons butter

1. Place each chicken breast half between 2 sheets of heavy-duty plastic wrap; pound to ½-inch thickness using a meat mallet or small heavy skillet.
2. Heat a large nonstick skillet over medium-high heat. Coat pan with cooking spray. Sprinkle chicken evenly with salt and pepper. Add chicken to pan. Cook 5 to 6 minutes on each side or until done. Remove chicken and drippings from pan; set aside, and keep warm.
3. Heat pan over medium-high heat; recoat pan with cooking spray. Add mushrooms. Coat mushrooms with cooking spray; cook 2 minutes or until tender, stirring frequently. Add wine and 3 tablespoons onions. Cook 30 seconds over high heat. Reduce heat; add butter, stirring until butter melts.
4. Add chicken and drippings to pan, stirring gently. Place chicken on a serving platter. Spoon mushroom sauce over chicken; sprinkle with remaining onions. **YIELD:** 4 servings (serving size: 1 chicken breast half and about ¼ cup mushroom sauce).

PER SERVING: CAL 291; FAT 8g (sat 4.2g); PRO 40.9g; CARB 6.2g; FIB 0.6g; SUG 3.3g; CHOL 114mg; IRON 1.6mg; SOD 303mg; CALC 40mg

Shiitake Mushrooms

The soft, brown, open cap of the shiitake mushroom lends itself to several cooking styles. Sautéing brings out the shiitake's strong smoky flavor, softens the texture to a velvety smoothness, and allows the mushroom to easily mingle with other ingredients.

Chicken Scaloppini

***PointsPlus* value:** 6

PREP: 10 minutes ■ **COOK:** 15 minutes

Scaloppini are cuts of meat that are pounded thin and then cooked to perfection in about 6 minutes. For a beautifully browned crust, make sure the pan and oil are hot—the chicken should hiss as it hits the pan.

4 (6-ounce) skinless, boneless chicken breast halves
1 large egg white
2 teaspoons water
½ cup Italian-seasoned breadcrumbs
2 teaspoons olive oil, divided
½ cup fat-free, lower-sodium chicken broth
1 tablespoon fresh lemon juice

1. Place each chicken breast half between 2 sheets of heavy-duty plastic wrap; pound to ½-inch thickness using a meat mallet or small heavy skillet.
2. Combine egg white and water in a shallow dish, stirring with a whisk. Place breadcrumbs in another shallow dish. Dip each chicken breast half in egg mixture; dredge in breadcrumbs.
3. Heat 1 teaspoon oil in a large nonstick skillet over medium-high heat. Add half of chicken to pan. Cook 3 minutes on each side or until golden. Transfer to a plate; cover and keep warm. Repeat procedure with remaining oil and chicken.
4. Add broth and lemon juice to pan, stirring to loosen browned bits. Cook, uncovered, over high heat 2 to 3 minutes or until reduced to ⅓ cup. Drizzle sauce over chicken. **YIELD:** 4 servings (serving size: 1 chicken breast half and about 1 tablespoon sauce).

PER SERVING: CAL 265; FAT 7g (sat 1.4g); PRO 37.4g; CARB 10.5g; FIB 0.5g; SUG 0.8g; CHOL 94mg; IRON 1.9mg; SOD 380mg; CALC 38mg

Smothered Green Chile Pepper Chicken

PointsPlus **value:** 7
PREP: 4 minutes ■ **COOK:** 35 minutes

Whole green chiles hug the chicken thighs and impart a mild, roasted flavor to both the meat and broth. The chiles used in this recipe come 3 per 4-ounce can.

8 (3-ounce) skinless, boneless chicken thighs
1 tablespoon fresh lime juice (about ½ lime)
3 tablespoons less-sodium taco seasoning
8 canned whole green chiles, drained
½ cup (2 ounces) shredded part-skim mozzarella cheese

1. Preheat oven to 400°.
2. Arrange chicken in an 8-inch square baking dish; squeeze lime juice evenly over chicken. Sprinkle evenly with taco seasoning.
3. Slice chiles lengthwise, cutting to, but not through, other side; open flat. Place 1 chile over each chicken thigh. Cover dish with foil; bake at 400° for 30 minutes. Sprinkle cheese evenly over chiles and chicken; bake, uncovered, an additional 5 minutes or until cheese melts. **YIELD:** 4 servings (serving size: 2 chicken thighs).

PER SERVING: CAL 301; FAT 15g (sat 5g); PRO 34.1g; CARB 4.7g; FIB 0.5g; SUG 0.5g; CHOL 120mg; IRON 2mg; SOD 574mg; CALC 116mg

Asian Barbecue Chicken

PointsPlus **value:** 8
PREP: 3 minutes ■ **COOK:** 10 minutes ■ **OTHER:** 5 minutes

Chinese hoisin sauce, mirin (a Japanese sweet rice wine), and Asian chili-garlic sauce create a quick, no-boil barbecue sauce that stands up to the dark meat of the chicken thighs.

¼ cup hoisin sauce
1½ tablespoons mirin (sweet rice wine)
1 teaspoon chili sauce with garlic (such as Hokan)
8 chicken thighs (about 2 pounds), skinned
Cooking spray
¼ cup presliced green onions

1. Prepare grill.
2. Combine first 3 ingredients in a large heavy-duty zip-top plastic bag; add chicken. Seal bag, and marinate 5 minutes. Remove chicken, and discard bag and marinade.
3. Place chicken on grill rack coated with cooking spray; grill 5 minutes on each side or until done. Transfer chicken to a serving platter, and sprinkle with green onions. **YIELD:** 4 servings (serving size: 2 chicken thighs).

PER SERVING: CAL 321; FAT 16.1g (sat 4.2g); PRO 31.7g; CARB 8.8g; FIB 0.2g; SUG 8g; CHOL 115mg; IRON 1.7mg; SOD 350mg; CALC 19mg

Zucchini

This summer squash has thin, edible skin and soft seeds. In peak form from June through late August, zucchini can be used in almost anything from salads and breads to gratins. Zucchini will keep in the refrigerator for about five days.

Smoked Sausage-and-Vegetable Pile-Up

***PointsPlus* value:** 8

PREP: 4 minutes ■ **COOK:** 11 minutes

Popular fast-food "all-in-one" bowls are loaded with fat and sodium. Our quick alternative is much healthier.

Cooking spray
7 ounces smoked turkey sausage, diagonally sliced
1 cup refrigerated prechopped onion
1 cup refrigerated prechopped tricolor bell pepper
1 cup refrigerated presliced zucchini
1 (20-ounce) package refrigerated garlic mashed potatoes (such as Simply Potatoes)
2 cups frozen whole-kernel corn

1. Heat a large nonstick skillet over medium-high heat. Coat pan with cooking spray. Add sausage; sauté 2 minutes or until browned. Remove from skillet; keep warm.
2. Return pan to heat; recoat pan with cooking spray. Add onion, bell pepper, and zucchini. Coat vegetables with cooking spray; sauté 5 minutes or until tender and beginning to brown.
3. While vegetables cook, heat potatoes according to package directions.
4. Add corn and cooked sausage to onion mixture. Sauté 4 minutes or until thoroughly heated. Serve sausage mixture over mashed potatoes. **YIELD:** 4 servings (serving size: 1 cup sausage and vegetables and ½ cup mashed potatoes).

PER SERVING: CAL 306; FAT 9g (sat 4.6g); PRO 12.9g; CARB 46.2g; FIB 6g; SUG 10.1g; CHOL 37mg; IRON 1.8mg; SOD 434mg; CALC 77mg

Turkey Cutlets with Orange Sauce

***PointsPlus* value:** 6

PREP: 4 minutes ■ **COOK:** 12 minutes

A dusting of cornstarch gives these cutlets a light crust that absorbs the sweet citrus sauce. Thin turkey cutlets cook very quickly, so be sure to watch them carefully.

1½ pounds turkey cutlets
½ teaspoon salt
¼ teaspoon freshly ground black pepper
1 tablespoon cornstarch
2 teaspoons olive oil, divided
1 cup orange juice
1 teaspoon brown sugar
3 tablespoons raisins

1. Sprinkle both sides of turkey with salt and pepper. Place cornstarch in a small metal sieve; sprinkle both sides of turkey evenly with cornstarch.
2. Heat 1 teaspoon oil in a large nonstick skillet over medium-high heat; add half of turkey to pan. Cook 2 minutes on each side or until lightly browned; remove from pan. Keep warm. Repeat procedure with remaining 1 teaspoon oil and remaining turkey.
3. Add orange juice, brown sugar, and raisins to pan; bring to a boil over high heat, and boil 2 minutes.
4. Return turkey to pan, turning to coat with sauce. **YIELD:** 4 servings (serving size: about 2 turkey cutlets and about 2 tablespoons sauce).

PER SERVING: CAL 263; FAT 3.3g (sat 0.4g); PRO 42.7g; CARB 15.6g; FIB 0.5g; SUG 10.9g; CHOL 68mg; IRON 2.5mg; SOD 443mg; CALC 12mg

Cheeseburger Penne

***PointsPlus* value:** 8

PREP: 4 minutes ■ **COOK:** 11 minutes

For an impressive presentation, spoon the assembled pasta ingredients into individual 6-inch cast-iron skillets before broiling.

2 cups uncooked multigrain penne (such as Barilla Plus)
1 (9-ounce) package frozen meatless burgers (such as Morningstar Farms Grillers Original)
Cooking spray
¾ cup refrigerated prechopped onion
1 (14.5-ounce) can fire roasted diced tomatoes with garlic (such as Hunt's)
1½ cups chopped tomato (1 large tomato)
½ teaspoon freshly ground black pepper
1¼ cups (5 ounces) 50% reduced-fat shredded extrasharp cheddar cheese (such as Cracker Barrel), divided
½ cup chopped dill pickle

1. Prepare grill.
2. Cook pasta according to package directions, omitting salt and fat; drain. Return pasta to pan, and keep warm.
3. Preheat broiler.
4. While pasta cooks, place burgers on grill rack coated with cooking spray. Grill 2 minutes; turn burgers over, and grill 2 minutes.
5. While burgers cook, heat a large cast-iron skillet over medium-high heat. Coat pan with cooking spray. Add onion; sauté 2 minutes. Stir in canned tomatoes, tomato, and pepper. Coarsely chop burgers; add to tomato mixture.
6. Stir tomato mixture and half of cheese into pasta, and spoon pasta mixture back into cast-iron skillet. Sprinkle with remaining half of cheese. Broil 1 to 2 minutes or until cheese melts. Sprinkle with chopped pickle. **YIELD:** 6 servings (serving size: about 1½ cups).

PER SERVING: CAL 320; FAT 10.4g (sat 4.1g); PRO 23g; CARB 33.8g; FIB 5.3g; SUG 5.5g; CHOL 17mg; IRON 2.2mg; SOD 650mg; CALC 232mg

Cheeseburger Penne

Spinach-Artichoke Pizza

***PointsPlus* value:** 2

PREP: 4 minutes ■ **COOK:** 10 minutes

Call your family to the table while this juicy veggie pizza is under the broiler so they will be ready to enjoy it right away. Baking the pizza crust in the oven while it preheats is the key to a crispy exterior.

1 (10-ounce) whole-wheat Italian cheese-flavored thin pizza crust (such as Boboli)
Olive oil–flavored cooking spray
½ cup marinara sauce
⅔ cup (2½ ounces) preshredded part-skim mozzarella cheese, divided
½ (5-ounce) package baby spinach (about 2 cups)
2 plum tomatoes, sliced (about 1 cup)
1 garlic clove, minced
½ cup canned artichoke hearts, drained and chopped
⅛ teaspoon crushed red pepper

1. Preheat oven to 450°.
2. While oven is preheating, place pizza crust directly on oven rack; bake 7 minutes or until crust is golden. Remove crust from oven, and place on a baking sheet.
3. Preheat broiler.
4. Coat pizza crust with cooking spray. Spread marinara sauce on crust, and sprinkle with ⅓ cup mozzarella cheese. Top with spinach, tomato, garlic, artichoke, and remaining ⅓ cup cheese.
5. Broil pizza 3 minutes or until cheese melts. Sprinkle with red pepper, and serve immediately. **YIELD:** 6 servings (serving size: 1 slice).

PER SERVING: CAL 189; FAT 5.4g (sat 2.9g); PRO 9.4g; CARB 5.5g; FIB 4.8g; SUG 2g; CHOL 6.8mg; IRON 1.5mg; SOD 442mg; CALC 149mg

Ravioli with Sun-Dried Tomato Cream Sauce

***PointsPlus* value:** 8

PREP: 4 minutes ■ **COOK:** 8 minutes

Use the pasta that steams in the microwave to avoid the step of bringing a large pot of water to a boil before cooking.

1 (18-ounce) package frozen steam-n-eat small cheese ravioli (such as Rosetto)
2 teaspoons olive oil
1 (8-ounce) package baby portobello mushrooms, quartered
½ cup coarsely chopped onion
½ teaspoon all-purpose flour
½ cup plus 2 tablespoons half-and-half
2 tablespoons sun-dried tomato pesto (such as Classico)
¼ teaspoon salt
¼ teaspoon pepper
¼ cup (1 ounce) shaved fresh Asiago cheese
Basil leaves (optional)

1. Cook ravioli in microwave according to package directions.
2. While ravioli cooks, heat oil in a large nonstick skillet over medium-high heat. Add mushrooms and onion; sauté 3 to 4 minutes or until richly browned. Combine flour and next 4 ingredients in a small bowl, stirring until smooth. Add to pan, stirring well. Cook over medium-low heat 2 minutes or until mixture thickens slightly.
3. Divide cooked ravioli evenly among 4 shallow bowls or plates; spoon mushroom mixture evenly over ravioli. Sprinkle cheese evenly over each serving; garnish with basil, if desired. **YIELD:** 4 servings (serving size: 13 ravioli, about ½ cup mushroom sauce, and 1 tablespoon cheese).

PER SERVING: CAL 306; FAT 9g (sat 3.8g); PRO 13.8g; CARB 41.5g; FIB 3.1g; SUG 6.6g; CHOL 21mg; IRON 2.9mg; SOD 583mg; CALC 199mg

Ravioli with Sun-Dried Tomato Cream Sauce

Sweet Grape Tomato and
White Bean Pasta

Sweet Grape Tomato and White Bean Pasta

PointsPlus **value:** 7

PREP: 1 minute ■ **COOK:** 14 minutes

Navy beans bump up the protein in this satisfying and healthy one-dish supper that's brimming with the tastes of summer.

1¾ cups uncooked multigrain penne (such as Barilla Plus)
1 tablespoon extra-virgin olive oil
2 cups halved grape tomatoes
2 garlic cloves, minced
1 cup chopped bottled roasted red bell peppers
½ (15-ounce) can navy beans, rinsed and drained
3 cups fresh baby spinach
¼ cup torn basil leaves
2 teaspoons balsamic vinegar
½ teaspoon salt
¼ cup (1 ounce) grated fresh Parmesan cheese

1. Cook pasta according to package directions, omitting salt and fat.
2. While pasta cooks, heat oil in a large nonstick skillet over medium-high heat. Add tomatoes; cook 3 minutes or until skins begin to wrinkle and burst. Add garlic; cook 1 minute, stirring constantly. Add bell pepper, beans, and spinach; cook 3 minutes or until spinach is slightly wilted. Stir in basil, vinegar, salt, and pasta. Cook 2 minutes or until thoroughly heated. Sprinkle evenly with cheese. **YIELD:** 4 servings (serving size: 1½ cups pasta and 1 tablespoon cheese).

PER SERVING: CAL 269; FAT 7g (sat 1.6g); PRO 12.3g; CARB 45.5g; FIB 8.3g; SUG 3.7g; CHOL 5mg; IRON 2.9mg; SOD 647mg; CALC 161mg

Grape tomatoes

These tiny tomatoes have an elliptical shape, similar to a grape. They have a more intense sweetness than cherry tomatoes, balanced by a subtle acidity. For the best flavor, look for grape tomatoes that are no larger than an inch in diameter. If they're larger, they'll have a higher water content and a diluted taste.

Spicy Vegetable Fried Rice

PointsPlus **value:** 7

PREP: 2 minutes ■ **COOK:** 9 minutes

The crushed red pepper adds a hint of heat to the Asian favorite. If you're sensitive to spices, simply omit it.

1½ cups frozen broccoli stir-fry (such as Birds Eye)
1 cup frozen shelled edamame (green soybeans)
Cooking spray
½ cup egg substitute
2 teaspoons dark sesame oil
2 teaspoons bottled minced garlic
¼ teaspoon crushed red pepper
2 (8.8-ounce) packages precooked whole-grain brown rice (such as Uncle Ben's Ready Rice)
2½ tablespoons lower-sodium soy sauce
Toasted sesame seeds (optional)
Sliced green onions (optional)

1. Combine broccoli stir-fry and edamame in a microwave-safe bowl. Microwave at HIGH 2 minutes or until thawed; set aside.
2. While vegetables thaw, heat a large nonstick skillet over medium-high heat; coat pan with cooking spray. Add egg substitute; cook 2 minutes, stirring frequently, until scrambled. Remove from pan. Wipe pan with paper towels.
3. Heat sesame oil in pan over medium-high heat; add garlic and crushed red pepper. Cook 1 minute or until fragrant. Stir in vegetables and rice; cook 2 minutes or until thoroughly heated. Stir in soy sauce and reserved egg. Garnish with sesame seeds and onions, if desired. **YIELD:** 4 servings (serving size: about 1⅓ cups).

PER SERVING: CAL 289; FAT 8g (sat 0.8g); PRO 11.5g; CARB 42.6g; FIB 4g; SUG 0.9g; CHOL 0mg; IRON 2mg; SOD 447mg; CALC 35mg

Tijuana Black Beans and Rice

***PointsPlus* value:** 7

PREP: 8 minutes ■ **COOK:** 7 minutes

If queso quesadilla cheese is unavailable, substitute shredded Monterey Jack.

1 (8.8-ounce) package precooked whole-grain brown rice (such as Uncle Ben's Ready Rice)
1 tablespoon canola oil
½ cup vertically sliced red onion
3 garlic cloves, minced
1 (15-ounce) can no-salt-added black beans, drained
1 (14.5-ounce) can diced tomatoes with zesty mild green chiles (such as Del Monte)
⅓ cup chopped fresh cilantro
2 tablespoons fresh lime juice
¼ teaspoon salt
½ cup (2 ounces) crumbled queso quesadilla cheese
1 lime, cut into wedges

1. Cook rice according to package directions.
2. Heat oil in a large nonstick skillet over medium-high heat. Add onion, and sauté 3 minutes or until browned. Stir in garlic; sauté 1 minute. Add beans and tomatoes, and cook 2 minutes or until thoroughly heated. Stir in cilantro, lime juice, and salt. Serve bean mixture over rice. Sprinkle with cheese; serve with lime wedges. **YIELD:** 4 servings (serving size: ¾ cup bean mixture, ½ cup rice, and 2 tablespoons cheese).

PER SERVING: CAL 266; FAT 9.4g (sat 3g); PRO 10.5g; CARB 36.5g; FIB 5.8g; SUG 1.4g; CHOL 15mg; IRON 1.8mg; SOD 663mg; CALC 160mg

Queso Quesadilla

Queso quesadilla is a soft, mild, white cheese. It's popular throughout Mexico for both snacking and cooking, and it becomes soft and creamy when heated. Traditionally, this type of cheese is mixed into refried beans, melted between tortillas for a wonderfully creamy quesadilla, or melted into a queso dipping sauce.

Fluffy Egg White Omelet with Spinach and Goat Cheese

***PointsPlus* value:** 4

PREP: 3 minutes ■ **COOK:** 9 minutes

This wonderfully flavorful omelet is chock-full of tender spinach, fresh basil, and creamy goat cheese. Serve with sliced tomatoes.

6 large egg whites
2 teaspoons water
¼ teaspoon salt
¼ teaspoon freshly ground black pepper
¼ teaspoon garlic powder
⅛ teaspoon ground red pepper
2 tablespoons chopped fresh basil
Butter-flavored cooking spray
1 cup packed coarsely chopped fresh baby spinach
½ cup (2 ounces) crumbled goat cheese
Chopped fresh basil (optional)

1. Combine first 6 ingredients in a large bowl. Beat with a mixer at high speed until soft peaks form; fold in basil.
2. Heat a medium nonstick skillet over medium-low heat. Coat pan with cooking spray. Spread egg mixture evenly in pan. Cover and cook 7 minutes or until center is set.
3. Sprinkle spinach and goat cheese over half of omelet. Carefully loosen omelet with a spatula; fold in half. Cover and cook 1 minute. Gently slide omelet onto a serving platter. Cut omelet into 2 wedges; sprinkle with additional fresh basil, if desired. Serve immediately. **YIELD:** 2 servings (serving size: 1 wedge).

PER SERVING: CAL 162; FAT 8.9g (sat 5.9g); PRO 17.4g; CARB 3.3g; FIB 0.8g; SUG 1.5g; CHOL 22mg; IRON 1.1mg; SOD 625mg; CALC 106mg

Fluffy Egg White Omelet with
Spinach and Goat Cheese

salads

With this standout array of crisp main-dish and side salads, dinner possibilities are endless and—best of all—delicious.

Chicken-Strawberry Salad with Goat Cheese-Pistachio Croutons

***PointsPlus* value:** 6

PREP: 4 minutes ■ **COOK:** 6 minutes

Striking in color and boasting fresh flavor, this delightful salad is crowned with pistachio-studded rounds of goat cheese.

4 (4-ounce) chicken cutlets
¼ teaspoon salt
¼ teaspoon freshly ground black pepper
⅓ cup strawberry balsamic vinaigrette (such as Maple Grove Farms), divided
Cooking spray
½ (4-ounce) log herbed goat cheese
2 tablespoons finely chopped pistachios
2 (5-ounce) packages organic salad greens with herbs (such as Fresh Express)
2 cups sliced strawberries

1. Prepare grill.
2. Sprinkle chicken with salt and pepper; brush with 2 tablespoons vinaigrette. Place chicken on grill rack coated with cooking spray; grill 3 to 4 minutes on each side or until done.
3. While chicken cooks, roll goat cheese in chopped nuts; cut into 8 slices.
4. Cut chicken into thin strips; place in a large bowl. Add greens, strawberries, and remaining dressing; toss well. Divide salad evenly among 4 plates; top each serving with 2 goat cheese rounds. **YIELD:** 4 servings (serving size: 2½ cups salad mixture and 2 goat cheese rounds).

PER SERVING: CAL 242; FAT 6.5g (sat 2.6g); PRO 30.4g; CARB 15.4g; FIB 3.8g; SUG 9.5g; CHOL 71mg; IRON 1.9mg; SOD 419mg; CALC 41mg

Feta-Chicken Couscous Salad with Basil

***PointsPlus* value:** 5

PREP: 8 minutes ■ **COOK:** 2 minutes ■ **OTHER:** 5 minutes

Serve this salad with crispbreads and red pepper hummus for a light summer meal.

1¼ cups water
⅔ cup uncooked whole-wheat couscous
1 cup diced cooked chicken breast (such as Tyson)
¼ cup chopped fresh basil
3 tablespoons capers, rinsed and drained
1 tablespoon extra-virgin olive oil
1 teaspoon grated lemon rind
1 tablespoon fresh lemon juice
2 cups mixed baby salad greens
¼ cup (1 ounce) crumbled reduced-fat feta cheese

1. Bring 1¼ cups water to a boil in a medium saucepan. Add couscous; cover and let stand 5 minutes.
2. While couscous stands, combine chicken and next 5 ingredients in a large bowl, tossing gently to coat.
3. Fluff couscous with a fork. Add couscous, salad greens, and cheese to chicken mixture; toss gently to coat.
YIELD: 4 servings (serving size: 1 cup).

PER SERVING: CAL 208; FAT 7g (sat 1.8g); PRO 17.2g; CARB 20.7g; FIB 2.7g; SUG 0.8g; CHOL 33mg; IRON 1.1mg; SOD 366mg; CALC 56mg

Lemons

Whether using juice, lemon rind (zest), or slices, the acidity of lemon adds to the final balance of flavor in all types of food, from savory to sweet. Look for lemons with smooth, brightly colored skins that are heavy for their size. Store up to 2 to 3 weeks in the refrigerator. Allow lemons to come to room temperature before juicing to ensure that you get the most juice from each lemon.

Salmon-Spinach Salad with Rosemary-Mustard Vinaigrette

***PointsPlus* value:** 5

PREP: 4 minutes ■ **COOK:** 10 minutes

In this recipe, the tangy rosemary-mustard vinaigrette stands up to bold-flavored salmon and gently coats the tender baby spinach leaves. The salmon is best torn into substantial chunks before tossing with the cucumber-onion mixture.

4 (6-ounce) salmon fillets (about 1 inch thick)
Cooking spray
½ cup chopped red onion
½ cup chopped cucumber
2 tablespoons fresh lemon juice
1 tablespoon minced fresh rosemary
1 tablespoon stone-ground mustard
1 tablespoon light mayonnaise
½ teaspoon salt
¼ teaspoon freshly ground black pepper
1 (6-ounce) package fresh baby spinach

1. Preheat broiler.
2. Place fillets, skin sides down, on a broiler pan coated with cooking spray. Broil 10 minutes or until desired degree of doneness.
3. While salmon cooks, combine onion and next 7 ingredients in a medium bowl. Remove skin from salmon, and break fish into bite-sized pieces. Add salmon to onion mixture; toss well.
4. Place 1 cup spinach on each of 6 plates. Top evenly with salmon mixture. **YIELD:** 6 servings (serving size: 1 cup salmon mixture and 1 cup spinach).

PER SERVING: CAL 207; FAT 9.7g (sat 2.3g); PRO 25.2g; CARB 3.3g; FIB 1g; SUG 1g; CHOL 59mg; IRON 1.3mg; SOD 318mg; CALC 48mg

Salmon-Spinach Salad with Rosemary-Mustard Vinaigrette

Greek Tuna Salad on Pita Rounds

***PointsPlus* value:** 10

PREP: 7 minutes

This recipe comes together in less than 10 minutes. No need to serve bread or crackers alongside—it's a one-dish meal with the salad piled onto a hummus-topped pita base.

2 tablespoons chopped pitted kalamata olives
2 tablespoons chopped red onion
2 tablespoons fresh lemon juice
1 tablespoon extra-virgin olive oil
½ teaspoon freshly ground black pepper
1 (6.4-ounce) pouch albacore tuna in water (such as StarKist), drained and flaked
1 celery stalk, sliced
4 (6-inch) whole-wheat pitas
½ cup cucumber-dill hummus (such as Athenos)
1 cup shredded romaine lettuce
¼ cup (1 ounce) crumbled feta cheese

1. Combine first 7 ingredients in a medium bowl. Place pitas on 4 serving plates; spread each with 2 tablespoons hummus, and top each with ¼ cup lettuce. Top evenly with about ⅓ cup tuna mixture, and sprinkle each with 1 tablespoon cheese. **YIELD:** 4 servings (serving size: 1 tuna salad–topped pita).

PER SERVING: CAL 339; FAT 13.5g (sat 2.7g); PRO 20.3g; CARB 43.9g; FIB 5.9g; SUG 1.6g; CHOL 27mg; IRON 2.3mg; SOD 899mg; CALC 69mg

Macaroni Salad

***PointsPlus* value:** 4

PREP: 4 minutes ■ **COOK:** 11 minutes

Dijon mustard and cider vinegar add a zip to this salad that contrasts well with fresh, crunchy red onion and celery.

4 ounces uncooked multigrain elbow macaroni (such as Barilla PLUS)
¼ cup light mayonnaise
2 tablespoons fat-free sour cream
1 tablespoon Dijon mustard
1 tablespoon cider vinegar
¼ teaspoon salt
¼ teaspoon freshly ground black pepper
½ cup thinly sliced celery
¼ cup finely chopped red onion
1 (2-ounce) jar diced pimiento, drained

1. Cook pasta according to package directions, omitting salt and fat. Drain; rinse with cold water until cool. Drain.
2. While pasta cooks, combine mayonnaise and next 5 ingredients in a large bowl, stirring with a whisk. Stir in celery, onion, and pimiento. Add pasta, stirring gently until coated. Serve immediately, or cover and chill until ready to serve. **YIELD:** 5 servings (serving size: about ½ cup).

PER SERVING: CAL 142; FAT 4.9g (sat 0.8g); PRO 4.7g; CARB 19.4g; FIB 2.1g; SUG 2g; CHOL 5mg; IRON 1.3mg; SOD 311mg; CALC 27mg

Pot Sticker Salad

***PointsPlus* value:** 6
PREP: 2 minutes ■ **COOK:** 7 minutes

In order to control the sodium in this dish, we've substituted a light salad dressing packed with plenty of flavor for the sauce that comes with the pot stickers.

2 teaspoons dark sesame oil
1 (13-ounce) package frozen vegetable pot stickers (such as Ling Ling)
1 (6-ounce) package 5-lettuce blend salad greens (such as Fresh Express)
1 cup snow peas, trimmed and halved crosswise
1 cup refrigerated prechopped tricolor bell pepper
¾ cup packaged coleslaw
⅓ cup low-fat sesame-ginger dressing (such as Newman's Own)

1. Heat oil in a large nonstick skillet over medium-high heat. Discard sauce packet from pot stickers. Add pot stickers to pan; cook 6 minutes, turning occasionally until browned.
2. While pot stickers cook, combine salad greens and next 4 ingredients. Divide salad among 4 plates. Place 3 pot stickers in center of each salad. **YIELD:** 4 servings (serving size: about 1 cup salad and 3 pot stickers).

PER SERVING: CAL 226; FAT 5.6g (sat 0.6g); PRO 6.1g; CARB 37.9g; FIB 3.1g; SUG 8.8g; CHOL 0mg; IRON 1.9mg; SOD 593mg; CALC 40mg

Edamame Salad

***PointsPlus* value:** 4

PREP: 6 minutes ■ **COOK:** 7 minutes

You'll love the way fresh parsley and lemon juice brighten up the flavor of this simple salad.

- 4 cups frozen shelled edamame (green soybeans)
- 2 tablespoons minced fresh parsley
- 2 tablespoons fresh lemon juice
- 1 tablespoon olive oil
- ½ teaspoon freshly ground black pepper
- ⅛ teaspoon salt
- ½ cup (2 ounces) shredded fresh pecorino Romano cheese

1. Cook edamame in boiling water to cover 3 minutes. Drain and plunge into ice water; drain.
2. Combine parsley and next 4 ingredients in a medium bowl, stirring with a whisk. Add edamame, and toss well. Sprinkle with cheese. **YIELD:** 8 servings (serving size: ½ cup edamame salad and 1 tablespoon cheese).

PER SERVING: CAL 174; FAT 9.1g (sat 2g); PRO 13.8g; CARB 11.5g; FIB 5.8g; SUG 2.7g; CHOL 5mg; IRON 0.1mg; SOD 159mg; CALC 65mg

Edamame

Edamame (eh-dah-MAH-meh) are soybeans that are not fully mature. The bean pod looks like a large, fuzzy sugar snap pea. Whether fresh or frozen, this healthful legume adds fiber, vitamin K, and protein to any nutritious diet. Find edamame in your supermarket's frozen vegetable aisle, and use it for an extra boost in salads, pastas, and casseroles. It also makes a healthy, nutty-tasting snack.

Garbanzo and Avocado Salad

PointsPlus **value:** 5
PREP: 15 minutes

This oil-free salad is quick to assemble and can be made ahead—just be sure not to add the avocado until right before serving.

1 cup grape tomatoes, halved
½ cup chopped green onions (3 large onions)
2 tablespoons fresh lemon juice
2 medium garlic cloves, minced
2 (16-ounce) cans reduced-sodium garbanzo beans (such as Bush's), rinsed and drained
1 (4.5-ounce) can chopped green chiles, undrained
¼ teaspoon salt
¼ teaspoon freshly ground black pepper
1 small ripe avocado
¼ cup (1 ounce) crumbled feta cheese

1. Combine first 8 ingredients in a medium bowl. Peel and chop avocado. Add to garbanzo bean mixture; toss gently. Sprinkle with cheese. **YIELD:** 5 servings (serving size: 1 cup).

PER SERVING: CAL 183; FAT 7.8g (sat 1.3g); PRO 9.2g; CARB 25.9g; FIB 6.8g; SUG 2.9g; CHOL 5mg; IRON 2.4mg; SOD 387mg; CALC 72mg

Sweet and Spicy Slaw

PointsPlus **value:** 1
PREP: 10 minutes

What makes this colorful slaw stand out is its clean heat from the poblano chile. Serve it alongside grilled or roasted pork or chicken.

2 tablespoons "measures-like-sugar" calorie-free sweetener (such as Splenda)
2 tablespoons cider vinegar
2 teaspoons canola oil
½ teaspoon celery seed
¼ teaspoon salt
¼ teaspoon crushed red pepper
½ (16-ounce) package coleslaw
½ cup refrigerated preshredded carrot
½ medium-sized red bell pepper, thinly sliced and cut into 2-inch strips
½ medium poblano chile, thinly sliced and cut into 2-inch strips

1. Combine first 6 ingredients in a large bowl, stirring with a whisk. Add coleslaw and remaining ingredients; toss well. Serve immediately, or chill up to 1 hour. **YIELD:** 6 servings (serving size: about ¾ cup).

PER SERVING: CAL 32; FAT 1.7g (sat 0.1g); PRO 0.7g; CARB 4g; FIB 1.5g; SUG 2.1g; CHOL 0mg; IRON 0.3mg; SOD 130mg; CALC 22mg

Sweet Lemon-Mint-Pear Salad

PointsPlus **value:** 1
PREP: 9 minutes

Try serving this salad with Apricot-Lemon Chicken on page 37.

1 tablespoon sugar
3 tablespoons fresh lemon juice
2 teaspoons canola oil
4 cups packed baby spinach and spring greens mix
1 firm pear, thinly sliced
½ cup sliced red onion
¼ cup torn fresh mint leaves

1. Combine first 3 ingredients in a large bowl, stirring with a whisk. Add greens mix and remaining ingredients; toss well. Serve immediately. **YIELD:** 4 servings (serving size: 1½ cups).

PER SERVING: CAL 72; FAT 2g (sat 0.2g); PRO 1g; CARB 13g; FIB 2.3g; SUG 8.1g; CHOL 0mg; IRON 1mg; SOD 20mg; CALC 35mg

Pears

Perfectly ripe pears are sweet with a subtle, intoxicating perfume. To ripen, place pears on the kitchen counter in a brown paper bag, and check them daily. It may take three to five days for them to fully ripen. If the neck area yields to gentle thumb pressure, the pear is ready to eat or cook.

Strawberry Salad with Greens and Berry Vinaigrette

***PointsPlus* value:** 4
PREP: 12 minutes ■ **COOK:** 2 minutes

Raspberries, blackberries, or seedless grapes are delicious replacements for strawberries and blueberries.

¼ cup raspberry vinegar
1 tablespoon honey
2 teaspoons olive oil
¼ teaspoon freshly ground black pepper
⅛ teaspoon salt
1 small garlic clove, minced
4 cups mixed baby salad greens
1 cup sliced strawberries
⅓ cup blueberries
2 tablespoons sliced almonds, toasted

1. Combine raspberry vinegar and next 5 ingredients, stirring with a whisk.
2. Combine mixed baby greens, strawberries, blueberries, and almonds in a large bowl. Pour vinaigrette over greens mixture; toss to coat. **YIELD:** 4 servings (serving size: about 1¼ cups salad).

PER SERVING: CAL 134; FAT 6.4g (sat 1.7g); PRO 3.4g; CARB 17.8g; FIB 2.6g; SUG 12.8g; CHOL 6mg; IRON 0.8mg; SOD 123mg; CALC 81mg

Mixed Greens Salad with Classic Vinaigrette

***PointsPlus* value:** 2
PREP: 8 minutes

Radishes are a great source of fiber, vitamin C, and potassium. They add extra crispness to this garden salad.

¼ cup red wine vinegar
2 tablespoons olive oil
1 tablespoon minced shallots
1 tablespoon Dijon mustard
1 teaspoon sugar
⅛ teaspoon freshly ground black pepper
8 cups packed mixed salad greens
1½ cups matchstick-cut carrots
¾ cup thinly sliced radishes (about 4 small)
2 tablespoons chopped fresh basil

1. Combine red wine vinegar and next 5 ingredients, stirring with a whisk.
2. Combine salad greens, carrots, radishes, and basil in a large bowl. Pour vinaigrette over salad greens mixture; toss to coat. **YIELD:** 8 servings (serving size: about 1 cup).

PER SERVING: CAL 81; FAT 5.9g (sat 1.8g); PRO 2.6g; CARB 5.1g; FIB 1.5g; SUG 1.7g; CHOL 6mg; IRON 0.5mg; SOD 99mg; CALC 71mg

Cucumber-Cherry Tomato Salad

***PointsPlus* value:** 2
PREP: 12 minutes

English cucumbers naturally have fewer seeds than regular cucumbers. Because there's no need to seed them, they can be prepared faster. They're bigger than other varieties, and they usually come individually wrapped in plastic. Look for them at major grocery stores.

⅓ cup cider vinegar
2 teaspoons olive oil
1 garlic clove, minced
¼ teaspoon salt
¼ teaspoon Italian seasoning
¼ teaspoon freshly ground black pepper
1 English cucumber, thinly sliced
3 cups halved cherry tomatoes
2 tablespoons chopped red onion
¼ cup diced peeled avocado
2 tablespoons chopped fresh basil

1. Combine cider vinegar and next 5 ingredients in a large bowl, stirring with a whisk. Add cucumber, tomatoes, and red onion; toss gently to coat.
2. Stir in avocado and basil; chill until ready to serve. **YIELD:** 4 servings (serving size: 1½ cups).

PER SERVING: CAL 76; FAT 4.5g (sat 0.7g); PRO 1.6g; CARB 8.2g; FIB 2.3g; SUG 1.1g; CHOL 0mg; IRON 0.9mg; SOD 159mg; CALC 20mg

Cucumber–Cherry Tomato Salad

soups & sandwiches

Always quick and effortless to prepare, these soups and sandwiches will fit the bill for a comforting weeknight supper.

Italian Wedding Soup

***PointsPlus* value:** 5

PREP: 2 minutes ■ **COOK:** 13 minutes

1½ cups fat-free, lower-sodium beef broth
1 cup water
½ cup uncooked orzo (rice-shaped pasta)
Cooking spray
9 ounces mild turkey Italian sausage
1 (14.5-ounce) can petite-cut diced tomatoes with garlic and olive oil (such as Del Monte), undrained
¼ teaspoon freshly ground black pepper
1 (6-ounce) package fresh baby spinach
¼ cup (1 ounce) shaved fresh Parmesan cheese

1. Combine broth and water in a Dutch oven; cover and bring to a boil. Add orzo. Cook, uncovered, 6 to 8 minutes or until orzo is tender; do not drain.
2. While broth mixture comes to a boil, heat a large nonstick skillet over medium heat. Coat pan with cooking spray.
3. While skillet heats, remove casings from sausage, and quickly shape into 24 (1-inch) balls. Add meatballs to pan. Cook 6 minutes, browning on all sides. Drain well.
4. Add meatballs, tomatoes, and pepper to pasta mixture; return to a boil. Add spinach; cook 30 seconds, stirring until spinach wilts. Ladle soup evenly into 4 bowls. Top evenly with cheese. **YIELD:** 4 servings (serving size: 1½ cups soup and 1 tablespoon cheese).

PER SERVING: CAL 185; FAT 6.4g (sat 0.8g); PRO 12.75g; CARB 20.8g; FIB 2.4g; SUG 4.4g; CHOL 29mg; IRON 2.5mg; SOD 741mg; CALC 84mg

Beefy Corn and Black Bean Chili

PointsPlus **value:** 4
PREP: 1 minute ■ **COOK:** 27 minutes

This dish has the flavor and aroma of a chili that has simmered all day—and only you have to know it hasn't. Dress it up with a dollop of sour cream and sliced green onions, and serve it with store-bought corn bread from your supermarket's bakery.

1 pound ground round
2 teaspoons salt-free chili powder blend (such as The Spice Hunter)
1 (14-ounce) package frozen seasoned corn and black beans (such as Pictsweet)
1 (14-ounce) can fat-free, lower-sodium beef broth
1 (15-ounce) can seasoned tomato sauce for chili (such as Hunt's Family Favorites)
Reduced-fat sour cream (optional)
Sliced green onions (optional)

1. Combine beef and chili powder blend in a large Dutch oven. Cook 6 minutes over medium-high heat or until beef is browned, stirring to crumble. Drain and return to pan.
2. Stir in frozen corn mixture, broth, and tomato sauce; bring to a boil. Cover, reduce heat, and simmer 10 minutes. Uncover and simmer 5 minutes, stirring occasionally.
3. Ladle chili into bowls. Top each serving with sour cream and green onions, if desired. **YIELD:** 6 servings (serving size: about 1 cup).

PER SERVING: CAL 193; FAT 3g (sat 1g); PRO 20g; CARB 20g; FIB 3.4g; SUG 6.4g; CHOL 40mg; IRON 2mg; SOD 825mg; CALC 0mg

Egg and Garlic Soup

PointsPlus **value:** 2
PREP: 2 minutes ■ **COOK:** 13 minutes

Prepare this simple soup as a meal starter, or add a salad and bread for a light supper.

6 cups fat-free, lower-sodium chicken broth
6 fresh sage leaves
6 large garlic cloves, minced
3 large eggs, lightly beaten
⅛ teaspoon freshly ground black pepper
¼ cup thinly sliced green onions

1. Combine chicken broth and sage in a large saucepan. Bring to a boil; remove and discard sage leaves. Stir garlic into broth; reduce heat, and simmer, uncovered, 5 minutes.
2. While stirring broth mixture, pour eggs into broth in a slow, steady stream; remove from heat. Ladle soup into 4 bowls. Sprinkle evenly with pepper and green onions. **YIELD:** 4 servings (serving size: 1¼ cups).

PER SERVING: CAL 101; FAT 3.2g (sat 0.9g); PRO 11.2g; CARB 5.5g; FIB 1g; SUG 2.8g; CHOL 135mg; IRON 1.3mg; SOD 821mg; CALC 54mg

Tortelloni Soup with Spinach and Mushrooms

PointsPlus **value:** 4
PREP: 3 minutes ■ **COOK:** 13 minutes

Substitute smaller-shaped cheese tortellini, if tortelloni aren't available.

3½ cups fat-free, lower-sodium chicken broth
1½ cups water
1 (9-ounce) package refrigerated cheese and roasted garlic tortelloni (such as Buitoni)
Cooking spray
3 garlic cloves, minced
1 (8-ounce) package presliced mushrooms
1 (6-ounce) package fresh baby spinach
½ teaspoon freshly ground black pepper
⅛ teaspoon salt

1. Bring chicken broth and 1½ cups water to a boil in a Dutch oven. Stir in tortelloni, and cook according to package directions, omitting salt and fat. Do not drain.
2. While pasta cooks, heat a large nonstick skillet over medium-high heat. Coat pan with cooking spray. Add garlic and mushrooms. Cook 5 minutes; stir and cook 1 minute.
3. Stir mushroom mixture into tortelloni mixture. Bring to a boil over high heat; add spinach, pepper, and salt. Cook 1 minute or just until spinach wilts. Serve immediately. **YIELD:** 6 servings (serving size: about 1 cup).

PER SERVING: CAL 161; FAT 4.2g (sat 1.9g); PRO 7.8g; CARB 22.5g; FIB.7g; SUG 2.8g; CHOL 17mg; IRON 1.7mg; SOD 564mg; CALC 102mg

Butternut Squash and Apple Soup

***PointsPlus* value:** 3

PREP: 6 minutes ■ **COOK:** 9 minutes

Sautéed apple, onion, and garlic add a made-from-scratch flavor to boxed soup.

- 2 teaspoons olive oil
- 1¼ cups chopped peeled Granny Smith apple (1 medium)
- ¾ cup chopped Vidalia or other sweet onion
- 3 garlic cloves, minced
- ¾ cup fat-free, lower-sodium chicken broth
- 2 (18.3-ounce) containers golden butternut squash soup (such as Campbell's V8)
- ½ teaspoon freshly ground black pepper
- ¼ cup (1 ounce) shredded Parmigiano-Reggiano cheese

1. Heat oil in a Dutch oven over medium-high heat. Add apple and onion; sauté 5 minutes or until tender and lightly browned. Add garlic; sauté 1 minute. Stir in broth.

2. Process mixture with a hand-held blender (immersion blender) until smooth. Stir in butternut squash soup and pepper. Cook over medium heat until thoroughly heated. Ladle soup into bowls; sprinkle each serving evenly with cheese. **YIELD:** 6 servings (serving size: 1 cup soup and 2 teaspoons cheese).

PER SERVING: CAL 122; FAT 4.1g (sat 1.9g); PRO 4.2g; CARB 18.6g; FIB 2.9g; SUG 8.4g; CHOL 9mg; IRON 0.4mg; SOD 503mg; CALC 84mg

Black Bean Burgers

Black Bean Burgers

***PointsPlus* value:** 6

PREP: 10 minutes ■ **COOK:** 5 minutes

Accompany these high-fiber, Southwestern-flavored burgers with baked tortilla chips. The bean mixture may seem a little sticky, but the patties bind together nicely once they begin to cook.

1 (15-ounce) can black beans, rinsed and drained
⅓ cup dry breadcrumbs
2 tablespoons chopped fresh cilantro
¼ cup chopped green onions
1 garlic clove, minced
1 large egg
½ teaspoon chili powder
½ teaspoon ground cumin
⅛ teaspoon salt
2 teaspoons canola oil
4 green leaf lettuce leaves
4 (1.8-ounce) white-wheat hamburger buns (such as Nature's Own)
½ cup refrigerated fresh salsa

1. Place beans in a large bowl; partially mash with a potato masher. Stir in breadcrumbs and next 7 ingredients. Divide bean mixture into 4 equal portions, shaping each into a ½-inch-thick patty.
2. Heat oil in a large nonstick skillet over medium-high heat. Add patties to pan; cook 2 to 3 minutes on each side or until patties are browned.
3. Place 1 lettuce leaf on bottom half of each of 4 buns. Top with 1 patty, 2 tablespoons salsa, and top half of each bun. **YIELD:** 4 servings (serving size: 1 burger).

PER SERVING: CAL 248; FAT 6.5g (sat 1.2g); PRO 12.2g; CARB 41.4g; FIB 9.9g; SUG 3.5g; CHOL 53mg; IRON 4.7mg; SOD 740mg; CALC 313mg

Southwestern Portobello Burgers

***PointsPlus* value:** 7

PREP: 1 minute ■ **COOK:** 9 minutes

These veggie burgers get their heat from chipotle peppers, which are smoke-dried jalapeños. If you have a timid palette, reduce the chipotle chiles to 1 teaspoon.

4 (4-inch) portobello caps
Cooking spray
¼ teaspoon salt
¼ teaspoon freshly ground black pepper
4 (.7-ounce) slices reduced-fat cheddar cheese or 4 (.75-ounce) slices part-skim mozzarella cheese
4 (1.8-ounce) white-wheat hamburger buns (such as Nature's Own)
⅓ cup light mayonnaise
2 teaspoons chopped chipotle chiles canned in adobo sauce
1 teaspoon lemon rind
1 large garlic clove, minced
Lettuce leaves, tomato slices, avocado slices, red onion slices (optional)

1. Prepare grill.
2. Remove stems from mushroom caps. Coat mushroom caps with cooking spray; place, gill sides up, on grill rack coated with cooking spray. Grill 4 minutes; turn caps over. Grill 4 minutes or until tender. Sprinkle mushroom caps evenly with salt and pepper. During last minute of grilling, place cheese slices on top of mushroom caps; add buns to grill rack. Cover with grill lid; grill 1 minute or until cheese melts and buns are toasted.
3. While mushrooms cook, combine mayonnaise and next 3 ingredients. Spread mayonnaise evenly on buns; place one mushroom cap on bottom half of each bun. Arrange lettuce leaves, tomato, avocado, and onion on mushroom caps, if desired. Place top halves of buns on burgers. **YIELD:** 4 servings (serving size: 1 burger).

PER SERVING: CAL 261; FAT 13.1g (sat 4.7g); PRO 12g; CARB 28.4g; FIB 7g; SUG 3.5g; CHOL 20.8mg; IRON 3.3mg; SOD 793mg; CALC 401mg

Grilled Turkey Burgers

***PointsPlus* value:** 8

PREP: 5 minutes ■ **COOK:** 7 minutes

The addition of moistened breadcrumbs ensures that these grilled burgers are juicy and delicious. If desired, spread burgers with your choice from the flavored mayonnaises in the box below.

¼ cup dry breadcrumbs
2 tablespoons fat-free milk
2 large egg whites
1½ pounds ground turkey breast
2 teaspoons 25%-less-sodium Montreal chicken seasoning (such as McCormick Grill Mates)
¼ teaspoon freshly ground black pepper
Cooking spray
4 (1½-ounce) whole-wheat hamburger buns
Curly leaf lettuce leaves, tomato slices, and red onion slices (optional)

1. Prepare grill.
2. Combine first 3 ingredients in a large bowl. Add turkey, chicken seasoning, and pepper. Using hands, gently mix until blended. Divide mixture into 4 equal portions, shaping each into a ½-inch-thick patty.
3. Place patties on a grill rack coated with cooking spray. Grill patties 7 minutes or until done, turning after 4 minutes.
4. Place 1 patty on bottom half of each bun; top each patty with lettuce, tomato, and onion, if desired. Place top halves of buns on burgers. **YIELD:** 4 servings (serving size: 1 burger).

PER SERVING: CAL 314; FAT 4.4g (sat 0.4g); PRO 44g; CARB 27.8g; FIB 3.5g; SUG 4.5g; CHOL 60mg; IRON 3.3mg; SOD 460mg; CALC 67mg

Prosciutto and Sharp Provolone French Wheat Sandwiches

***PointsPlus* value:** 5

PREP: 10 minutes

We used sandwich-sized flatbreads for this trendy sandwich. If they are unavailable, substitute whole-wheat English muffins.

¼ cup light balsamic vinaigrette
1 garlic clove, finely minced
4 (1½-ounce) presliced whole-wheat sandwich thin flatbreads (such as Arnold Select 100% Whole Wheat Sandwich Thins)
4 (¼-inch-thick) slices tomato
16 large basil leaves
2 ounces thinly sliced prosciutto
4 (½-ounce) slices sharp provolone cheese
2 cups packed baby arugula
1 cup thinly sliced green bell pepper

1. Combine vinaigrette and garlic in a small bowl. Brush evenly on 1 side of each flatbread half. Top 4 bottom halves with 1 slice tomato, 4 basil leaves, ½ ounce prosciutto, 1 slice cheese, ½ cup arugula, and ¼ cup bell pepper. Top with remaining flatbread halves. **YIELD:** 4 servings (serving size: 1 sandwich).

PER SERVING: CAL 211; FAT 8.3g (sat 3.2g); PRO 12.7g; CARB 25.1g; FIB 6.9g; SUG 4g; CHOL 18mg; IRON 1.8mg; SOD 808mg; CALC 179mg

Chipotle Mayonnaise:

***PointsPlus* value:** 1

Combine ¼ cup light mayonnaise, 2 teaspoons minced chipotle chiles canned in adobo sauce, and 1 teaspoon adobo sauce in a small bowl, stirring until blended. **YIELD:** 5 servings (serving size: 1 tablespoon).

PER SERVING: CAL 44; FAT 4.3g (sat 0.8g); PRO 0g; CARB 1.3g; FIB 0.2g; SUG 0.2g; CHOL 4mg; IRON 0.1mg; SOD 324mg; CALC 2mg

Chili-Garlic Mayonnaise:

***PointsPlus* value:** 1

Combine ¼ cup light mayonnaise and 2 teaspoons chili sauce with garlic (such as Hokan) in a small bowl, stirring until blended. **YIELD:** 5 servings (serving size: 1 tablespoon).

PER SERVING: CAL 40; FAT 4.0g (sat 0.8g); PRO 0g; CARB 1g; FIB 0g; SUG 0.2g; CHOL 4mg; IRON 0mg; SOD 142mg; CALC 0mg

Chutney Mayonnaise:

***PointsPlus* value:** 1

Combine ¼ cup light mayonnaise, 1 tablespoon mango chutney (such as Major Grey), and ⅛ teaspoon curry powder or ground allspice in a small bowl, stirring until blended. **YIELD:** 5 servings (serving size: 1 tablespoon).

PER SERVING: CAL 45; FAT 4.0g (sat 0.8g); PRO 0.1g; CARB 2.2g; FIB 0.1g; SUG 1.2g; CHOL 4mg; IRON 0.1mg; SOD 97mg; CALC 1mg

Roast Beef Panini Sandwiches with Goat Cheese-Horseradish Spread

PointsPlus **value:** 9

PREP: 7 minutes ■ **COOK:** 7 minutes

The creamy and spicy spread transforms these simple roast beef sandwiches into something extraordinary. To prepare the sandwiches quickly, combine the ingredients for the spread, and begin assembling the sandwiches while the onion cooks.

1 small red onion, thinly sliced
Cooking spray
2 ounces goat cheese, softened
2 tablespoons light mayonnaise
2 tablespoons prepared horseradish
1 (8.5-ounce) whole-wheat baguette, halved lengthwise
2 tablespoons spicy brown mustard
⅔ pound thinly sliced low-sodium deli roast beef (such as Boar's Head)
2 cups arugula leaves

1. Preheat panini press or indoor electric grill.
2. Coat onion slices with cooking spray. Cook in panini press or indoor electric grill 4 to 5 minutes or until tender; remove from grill.
3. While onion cooks, combine goat cheese and next 2 ingredients in small bowl; stir until well blended.
4. Spread goat cheese mixture on top half of baguette. Spread mustard on bottom half of baguette; layer evenly with roast beef, grilled onion, and arugula. Replace top half of baguette. Cut baguette into 4 sandwiches. Cook sandwiches in panini press or indoor electric grill 3 to 4 minutes or until golden brown. **YIELD:** 4 servings (serving size: 1 sandwich).

PER SERVING: CAL 352; FAT 11g (sat 4.8g); PRO 29.5g; CARB 31.7g; FIB 2.1g; SUG 3.4g; CHOL 54mg; IRON 4.2mg; SOD 661mg; CALC 107mg

Asian Pork Wraps

Asian Pork Wraps

***PointsPlus* value:** 5

PREP: 6 minutes ■ **COOK:** 5 minutes

These overstuffed wraps boast an Asian-flavored pork mixture accented by crunchy water chestnuts.

1 tablespoon lower-sodium soy sauce
2 teaspoons dark sesame oil
¼ teaspoon salt
¼ teaspoon pepper
3 garlic cloves, pressed
3 (4-ounce) boneless loin pork chops, cut into thin strips
Cooking spray
1 (8-ounce) can diced water chestnuts, drained
1 cup shredded iceberg lettuce
4 (6-inch) 96% fat-free whole-wheat tortillas (such as Mission)
⅓ cup fresh cilantro leaves

1. Combine first 6 ingredients, tossing to coat pork. Heat a large nonstick skillet over medium-high heat. Coat pan with cooking spray. Add pork mixture; stir-fry 4 minutes or until pork is done. Stir in water chestnuts, and remove from heat.

2. Arrange lettuce evenly down center of each tortilla. Top with pork mixture and cilantro leaves; roll up. Secure with wooden picks. **YIELD:** 4 servings (serving size: 1 wrap).

PER SERVING: CAL 293; FAT 8.7g (sat 2.1g); PRO 20.7g; CARB 30.9g; FIB 4g; SUG 0.8g; CHOL 50mg; IRON 2.1mg; SOD 678mg; CALC 119mg

Greek Lentil Pitas with Tzatziki Sauce

***PointsPlus* value:** 5

PREP: 7 minutes ■ **COOK:** 7 minutes

Lentils, garlic, cumin, and lemon rind combine in mock falafel patties that are tucked into pita halves and topped with a refreshing cucumber-yogurt sauce.

1 lemon
3 garlic cloves, divided
½ teaspoon salt, divided
½ teaspoon freshly ground black pepper, divided
½ cup panko (Japanese breadcrumbs)
1 teaspoon ground cumin
1 (15-ounce) can lentils, rinsed and drained
1 large egg
Olive oil–flavored cooking spray
½ cup fat-free Greek yogurt
½ cup chopped seeded peeled cucumber
1 tablespoon chopped fresh cilantro
2 (6-inch) whole-wheat pitas, cut in half
Green leaf lettuce leaves, tomato slices, red onion slices (optional)

1. Grate rind and squeeze juice from lemon to measure 1 teaspoon rind and 1 tablespoon juice. Drop 2 garlic cloves through food chute with processor on. Process until minced. Add lemon rind, ¼ teaspoon salt, ¼ teaspoon pepper, panko, and next 3 ingredients. Process until blended. Divide lentil mixture into 8 equal portions. Shape each portion into a ¼-inch-thick patty.

2. Heat a large nonstick skillet over medium-high heat. Coat pan with cooking spray. Add patties; cook 3 minutes on each side or until patties are browned.

3. While patties cook, mince remaining garlic clove. Combine minced garlic, lemon juice, remaining ¼ teaspoon salt, remaining ¼ teaspoon pepper, yogurt, cucumber, and cilantro in a medium bowl.

4. Place 2 patties in each pita half; top with lettuce, tomato, and onion, if desired. Spoon 3 tablespoons tzatziki sauce over patties in each pita half. **YIELD:** 4 servings (serving size: 1 pita half).

PER SERVING: CAL 202; FAT 2.2g (sat 0.4g); PRO 13.1g; CARB 33.4g; FIB 8.6g; SUG 4.3g; CHOL 53mg; IRON 0.8mg; SOD 552mg; CALC 112mg

side dishes

Complement your favorite main dishes with these super-easy vegetable, grain, and pasta side dishes.

Kale with Cranberries, Apricots, and Almonds

***PointsPlus* value:** 2

PREP: 5 minutes ■ **COOK:** 14 minutes

Chewy kale, tangy cranberries, and sweet apricots combine to make a healthy and nutritious side dish.

- ½ cup water
- 1 tablespoon balsamic vinegar
- 1 pound kale, trimmed and cut into 2-inch pieces (about 12 cups)
- ¼ cup slivered almonds
- ¼ cup dried cranberries
- ¼ cup finely chopped dried apricots

1. Combine water and vinegar in a large Dutch oven; bring to a boil over medium-high heat. Add kale; cover, reduce heat, and simmer 12 minutes or until tender and liquid almost evaporates, stirring occasionally.
2. While kale cooks, heat a medium nonstick skillet over medium-high heat. Add almonds; cook 4 minutes or until toasted, stirring constantly.
3. Add toasted almonds, cranberries, and apricots to kale; toss gently to combine. Serve immediately. **YIELD:** 6 servings (serving size: ¾ cup).

PER SERVING: CAL 86; FAT 2.7g (sat 0.3g); PRO 3.1g; CARB 13.9g; FIB 1.8g; SUG 3.4g; CHOL 0mg; IRON 1.3mg; SOD 23mg; CALC 128mg

Spinach with Raisins and Pine Nuts

***PointsPlus* value:** 2

PREP: 4 minutes ■ **COOK:** 7 minutes

This side dish coupled with a rotisserie chicken and whole-grain couscous make a quick weeknight meal with a Mediterranean flair.

1 tablespoon olive oil
½ cup thinly sliced red onion
2 (6-ounce) packages fresh baby spinach
¼ cup golden raisins
⅜ teaspoon salt, divided
2 tablespoons pine nuts, toasted
¼ teaspoon freshly ground black pepper

1. Heat oil in a Dutch oven over medium-high heat. Add onion; sauté 3 minutes or until browned. Stir in spinach, raisins, and ⅛ teaspoon salt; cook 2 to 4 minutes or until spinach wilts, stirring occasionally.
2. Add pine nuts, pepper, and remaining ¼ teaspoon salt to spinach mixture; toss gently to combine. Serve immediately. **YIELD:** 6 servings (serving size: ½ cup).

PER SERVING: CAL 77; FAT 4.5g (sat 0.5g); PRO 2.4g; CARB 9g; FIB 1.8g; SUG 5.3g; CHOL 0mg; IRON 1.9mg; SOD 191mg; CALC 63mg

Balsamic Sautéed Spinach

***PointsPlus* value:** 1

PREP: 2 minutes ■ **COOK:** 10 minutes

Rich in iron and vitamins A and C, this quick side dish is a flavorful addition to any meal.

2 teaspoons olive oil
1 garlic clove, minced
4 (6-ounce) packages fresh baby spinach
1 tablespoon balsamic vinegar

1. Heat oil in a large nonstick skillet over medium-high heat. Add garlic; sauté 30 seconds. Add 1 package of spinach; cook 2 minutes or until spinach begins to wilt, stirring frequently. Add remaining spinach, 1 package at a time, stirring frequently until spinach wilts and mixture is hot. Stir in vinegar; serve immediately. **YIELD:** 6 servings (serving size: ½ cup).

PER SERVING: CAL 43; FAT 2g (sat 0.3g); PRO 3.3g; CARB 4.7g; FIB 2.5g; SUG 0.8g; CHOL 0mg; IRON 3.1mg; SOD 90mg; CALC 114mg

Broccoli Florets with Creamy Curry Mustard Sauce

***PointsPlus* value:** 1

PREP: 5 minutes ■ **COOK:** 8 minutes

7 cups broccoli florets (about 1 pound)
¼ cup light mayonnaise
2 tablespoons fat-free milk
1 tablespoon honey
1½ teaspoons prepared mustard
¼ teaspoon curry powder
¼ teaspoon salt

1. Steam broccoli, covered, 8 minutes or until tender. Drain.
2. While broccoli cooks, combine mayonnaise and next 5 ingredients in a small saucepan, stirring with a whisk. Cook over medium heat 2 minutes or until thoroughly heated and smooth, stirring frequently (do not boil). Spoon sauce over broccoli. **YIELD:** 6 servings (serving size: 1 cup broccoli and about 1½ tablespoons sauce).

PER SERVING: CAL 44; FAT 0.9g (sat 0g); PRO 2.5g; CARB 8.5g; FIB 2.2g; SUG 3.2g; CHOL 0mg; IRON 0.7mg; SOD 222mg; CALC 43mg

Roasted Asparagus with Goat Cheese

***PointsPlus* value:** 1

PREP: 2 minutes ■ **COOK:** 10 minutes

This dish is great because it serves up so much flavor and is unbelievably fast and easy.

1 pound asparagus, trimmed
Olive oil–flavored cooking spray
⅛ teaspoon salt
⅛ teaspoon freshly ground black pepper
¼ cup (1 ounce) crumbled goat cheese

1. Preheat oven to 450°.
2. Spread asparagus on a large rimmed baking sheet coated with cooking spray. Coat asparagus with cooking spray. Sprinkle evenly with salt and pepper.
3. Bake asparagus at 450° for 10 to 12 minutes or until crisp-tender. Sprinkle with goat cheese, and serve immediately. **YIELD:** 4 servings (serving size: ¼ of asparagus and 1 tablespoon goat cheese).

PER SERVING: CAL 43; FAT 2.3g (sat 1.5g); PRO 3.1g; CARB 3.3g; FIB 1.5g; SUG 1.7g; CHOL 6mg; IRON 0.4mg; SOD 109mg; CALC 37mg

Shredded Brussels Sprouts with Pecans

***PointsPlus* value:** 3

PREP: 5 minutes ■ **COOK:** 5 minutes

Substituting white balsamic vinegar for regular balsamic will preserve the bright color of the sprouts. Clean and slice Brussels sprouts ahead, and store them in a zip-top bag, if desired.

1 pound Brussels sprouts, trimmed
Cooking spray
½ cup vertically sliced red onion
1 tablespoon balsamic vinegar
1 tablespoon brown sugar
¼ teaspoon salt
¼ teaspoon pepper
¼ cup chopped pecans

1. Thinly slice Brussels sprouts (they will look shredded).
2. Heat a large nonstick skillet over medium-high heat. Coat pan with cooking spray. Add Brussels sprouts and onion to pan. Sauté 3 minutes or just until tender. Add vinegar and remaining ingredients; cook 1 minute or until sugar dissolves. Serve immediately. **YIELD:** 4 servings (serving size: about ⅔ cup).

PER SERVING: CAL 123; FAT 5.7g (sat 0.5g); PRO 4.7g; CARB 16.7g; FIB 5.3g; SUG 2.9g; CHOL 0mg; IRON 1.9mg; SOD 178mg; CALC 61mg

Curried Roasted Cauliflower with Greek Yogurt Sauce

***PointsPlus* value:** 2
PREP: 2 minutes ■ **COOK:** 13 minutes

4	cups cauliflower florets
1	tablespoon olive oil
¼	teaspoon curry powder
½	teaspoon kosher salt
¼	teaspoon freshly ground black pepper
½	cup plain fat-free Greek yogurt
1	tablespoon fresh lemon juice
½	teaspoon sugar
1	garlic clove, pressed
2	tablespoons chopped fresh flat-leaf parsley

1. Preheat oven to 475°.
2. Arrange cauliflower on a jelly-roll pan. Combine olive oil and curry powder in a small bowl. Microwave at HIGH 30 seconds; pour over cauliflower, and toss well. Sprinkle with salt and pepper. Bake at 475° for 13 minutes or until roasted.
3. While cauliflower roasts, combine yogurt and next 3 ingredients in a small bowl. Spoon sauce over roasted cauliflower; sprinkle with parsley. **YIELD:** 4 servings (serving size: about ¾ cup cauliflower and 2 tablespoons yogurt sauce).

PER SERVING: CAL 77; FAT 3.5g (sat 0.5g); PRO 5g; CARB 7.8g; FIB 2.7g; SUG 4.2g; CHOL 0mg; IRON 0.6mg; SOD 238mg; CALC 65mg

Steamed Cauliflower with Cheddar Sauce

***PointsPlus* value:** 2
PREP: 5 minutes ■ **COOK:** 10 minutes

Adding butter at the very end makes this cheddar sauce rich and silky smooth.

5 cups cauliflower florets
4 teaspoons all-purpose flour
¼ teaspoon salt
⅛ teaspoon ground red pepper
⅔ cup fat-free milk
½ cup (2 ounces) reduced-fat shredded sharp cheddar cheese
2 teaspoons butter

1. Steam cauliflower, covered, 5 minutes or until tender. Keep warm.
2. Place flour, salt, and red pepper in a small saucepan; gradually add milk, stirring with a whisk until blended. Bring to a boil over medium-high heat, stirring constantly. Reduce heat; cook 4 minutes or until thick, stirring constantly. Remove from heat; add cheese, stirring until smooth. Add butter, stirring until butter melts. **YIELD:** 6 servings (serving size: ½ cup cauliflower and 2 tablespoons sauce).

PER SERVING: CAL 86; FAT 4g (sat 2.4g); PRO 6.1g; CARB 8.4g; FIB 2.9g; SUG 3.9g; CHOL 11mg; IRON 0.5mg; SOD 140mg; CALC 127mg

Herb-Roasted Acorn Squash

***PointsPlus* value:** 2
PREP: 6 minutes ■ **COOK:** 24 minutes

Acorn squash is a winter squash that's ribbed and shaped like a giant acorn. It has dark green skin and orange flesh. The sweetness of the squash pairs well with savory fresh herbs.

2 tablespoons chopped fresh parsley
2 teaspoons chopped fresh oregano
2 teaspoons chopped fresh thyme
¼ teaspoon kosher salt
⅛ teaspoon freshly ground black pepper
1 acorn squash (about 1½ pounds)
Olive oil–flavored cooking spray

1. Preheat oven to 450°.
2. Combine parsley and next 4 ingredients in a small bowl.
3. Cut squash in half lengthwise. Discard seeds and membranes. Cut each half lengthwise into 4 wedges. Place wedges, cut sides up, in a large roasting pan. Coat squash with cooking spray; top with parsley mixture. Bake at 450° for 24 minutes, turning squash after 12 minutes. **YIELD:** 4 servings (serving size: 2 wedges).

PER SERVING: CAL 70; FAT 0.2g (sat 0g); PRO 1.5g; CARB 18.1g; FIB 2.7g; SUG 3.8g; CHOL 0mg; IRON 1.4mg; SOD 124mg; CALC 64mg

Maple-Roasted Carrots and Parsnips

***PointsPlus* value:** 4
PREP: 16 minutes ■ **COOK:** 45 minutes

For the best browning, spread the carrots and parsnips in a single layer, and stir only once during roasting.

1 pound carrots, cut into 1¼-inch sticks (about 3 cups)
1 pound parsnips, cut into 1¼-inch sticks (about 3 cups)
2 tablespoons maple syrup
1½ tablespoons olive oil
¼ teaspoon salt
¼ teaspoon freshly ground black pepper
1 tablespoon balsamic vinegar

1. Preheat oven to 425°.
2. Combine first 6 ingredients in a large bowl; toss to coat. Arrange vegetable mixture in a single layer on a foil-lined jelly-roll pan. Bake at 425° for 45 minutes or until browned and crisp, turning once. Drizzle with vinegar, and serve immediately. **YIELD:** 5 servings (serving size: ⅔ cup).

PER SERVING: CAL 165; FAT 4.7g (sat 0.6g); PRO 2g; CARB 31g; FIB 4.4g; SUG 9.5g; CHOL 0mg; IRON 0.9mg; SOD 191mg; CALC 69mg

Parsnips

A parsnip resembles a pale carrot but tends to taper more. Parsnips are available year-round, but their peak seasons are fall and winter. When purchasing, select firm parsnips with even, creamy beige skins that are free of spots. Store parsnips loosely covered in plastic wrap or in a zip-top plastic bag in your refrigerator's vegetable crisper drawer for 2 to 3 weeks.

Vegetable Ribbons with Mustard Butter

PointsPlus **value:** 1

PREP: 10 minutes ■ **COOK:** 4 minutes

Graceful ribbons of yellow squash and zucchini make a pretty side dish that's surprisingly easy to make. Just use a vegetable peeler to cut long paper-thin strips of each vegetable.

- 3 small yellow squash
- 2 small zucchini
- 2 teaspoons butter
- 2 teaspoons Dijon mustard
- ¼ teaspoon salt
- ⅛ teaspoon freshly ground black pepper

1. Cut yellow squash and zucchini into very thin slices using a vegetable peeler.
2. Place thinly sliced vegetables and butter in a microwave-safe bowl. Cover dish with a double layer of moistened paper towels. Microwave at HIGH 3 minutes. Add mustard, salt, and pepper, tossing to coat. Cover with moistened paper towels, and cook at HIGH 1 minute or until crisp-tender. **YIELD:** 4 servings (serving size: about ½ cup).

PER SERVING: CAL 38; FAT 2.1g (sat 1.2g); PRO 1.4g; CARB 4.3g; FIB 1.3g; SUG 2.2g; CHOL 5mg; IRON 0.4mg; SOD 226mg; CALC 18mg

Italian Zucchini and Tomatoes

PointsPlus **value:** 2

PREP: 4 minutes ■ **COOK:** 11 minutes

This versatile side is delicious with chicken or spooned over rice or polenta and sprinkled with Parmesan cheese.

- 2 medium zucchini
- 2 teaspoons olive oil
- 1 cup refrigerated presliced onion, cut in half
- 2 garlic cloves, minced
- 1 (14.5-ounce) can diced tomatoes with basil, garlic, and oregano, undrained

1. Cut zucchini in half lengthwise; cut halves crosswise into ¼-inch-thick slices.
2. Heat oil in a large nonstick skillet over medium-high heat. Add zucchini, onion, and garlic; sauté 8 minutes or until tender. Add tomato; cook 2 minutes or until thoroughly heated, stirring occasionally. **YIELD:** 4 servings (serving size: ¾ cup).

PER SERVING: CAL 90; FAT 2.5g (sat 0.4g); PRO 2.5g; CARB 15.5g; FIB 2.3g; SUG 9.3g; CHOL 0mg; IRON 1.1mg; SOD 437mg; CALC 78mg

Roasted Potato Wedges

PointsPlus **value:** 3

PREP: 3 minutes ■ **COOK:** 20 minutes

Tender baby Yukon gold potatoes need little fussing over. Simply season them with fresh rosemary and grated Parmesan-Romano cheese, and roast them for an easy side.

- 1 pound baby Yukon gold potatoes, halved
- 2 teaspoons olive oil
- 1 teaspoon chopped fresh rosemary
- 2 tablespoons grated Parmesan-Romano cheese blend
- ¼ teaspoon kosher salt
- Cooking spray

1. Preheat oven to 475°.
2. Combine potato and oil in a medium bowl, tossing to coat. Combine rosemary, cheese, and salt in a large zip-top plastic bag; add potato, tossing to coat. Place potato on a jelly-roll pan coated with cooking spray. Bake at 475° for 20 minutes or until browned and crispy. **YIELD:** 4 servings (serving size: about ¾ cup).

PER SERVING: CAL 121; FAT 3.6g (sat 1.1g); PRO 3.8g; CARB 19.5g; FIB 2.1g; SUG 1.1g; CHOL 4mg; IRON 1mg; SOD 193mg; CALC 59mg

Pan-Roasted Herbed Mushrooms

PointsPlus **value:** 2

PREP: 3 minutes ■ **COOK:** 10 minutes

Minimal stirring promotes a rich browning of the mushrooms and produces maximum flavor in this savory side for steak or other grilled meat. Cremini mushrooms vary in size, from large ones that need quartering to small ones that don't need cutting at all. Make sure the pieces are uniform for even cooking.

Cooking spray
2 (8-ounce) packages fresh cremini mushrooms, halved
2 garlic cloves, minced
¼ cup Marsala
1 tablespoon chopped fresh thyme
1 tablespoon butter
¼ teaspoon salt
¼ teaspoon freshly ground black pepper

1. Heat a large nonstick skillet over medium-high heat. Coat pan with cooking spray. Add mushrooms; cook 6 minutes, without stirring. Add garlic; cook, stirring constantly, 2 minutes. Add Marsala and remaining ingredients, stirring until butter melts. **YIELD:** 4 servings (serving size: ½ cup).

PER SERVING: CAL 72; FAT 3g (sat 1.8g); PRO 3g; CARB 6.4g; FIB 0.8g; SUG 3.1g; CHOL 8mg; IRON 0.6mg; SOD 176mg; CALC 28mg

Sweet Potatoes with Orange-Thyme Butter

Sweet Potatoes with Orange-Thyme Butter

***PointsPlus* value:** 5
PREP: 3 minutes ■ **COOK:** 8 minutes

Get a healthy dose of vitamins A and C with these herb- and citrus-infused potatoes.

4 (6-ounce) sweet potatoes
2 tablespoons butter, softened
2 teaspoons grated orange rind
1 teaspoon chopped fresh thyme
¼ teaspoon freshly ground black pepper
⅛ teaspoon salt

1. Scrub potatoes, and place in a medium bowl (do not pierce potatoes with a fork). Cover bowl with plastic wrap (do not allow plastic wrap to touch food); vent. Microwave at HIGH 8 minutes or until done.
2. While potatoes cook, combine butter and remaining 4 ingredients in a small bowl.
3. Cut each potato in half lengthwise; fluff with a fork. Top each potato evenly with butter mixture. **YIELD:** 4 servings (serving size: 1 sweet potato and 2¼ teaspoons butter).

PER SERVING: CAL 198; FAT 6g (sat 3.6g); PRO 2.7g; CARB 34.6g; FIB 5.3g; SUG 7.1g; CHOL 15mg; IRON 1.1mg; SOD 207mg; CALC 56mg

Mushroom and Zucchini Orzo

***PointsPlus* value:** 5
PREP: 6 minutes ■ **COOK:** 12 minutes

Diced zucchini and sliced mushrooms add garden-fresh flavor to this warm pasta dish; it makes a great accompaniment for grilled chicken or fish.

1 cup uncooked orzo (rice-shaped pasta)
Cooking spray
1 cup sliced mushrooms
1 cup diced zucchini
1 tablespoon butter
½ teaspoon dried oregano
¼ teaspoon salt
¼ teaspoon freshly ground black pepper

1. Cook orzo according to package directions, omitting salt and fat. Drain and keep warm.
2. While orzo cooks, heat a large nonstick skillet over medium-high heat. Coat pan with cooking spray. Add mushrooms and zucchini; sauté 6 minutes or until tender and browned.
3. Combine orzo, mushroom mixture, and remaining ingredients in a large bowl, tossing gently. **YIELD:** 4 servings (serving size: ¾ cup).

PER SERVING: CAL 197; FAT 4g (sat 1.8g); PRO 6.3g; CARB 34.2g; FIB 2.1g; SUG 3.6g; CHOL 8mg; IRON 0.3mg; SOD 171mg; CALC 11mg

Almond-Ginger Rice

***PointsPlus* value:** 3
PREP: 1 minute ■ **COOK:** 20 minutes

While the rice cooks, you can toast the almonds in a 350° oven for 5 to 6 minutes or just until lightly browned. Serve this easy accompaniment alongside fish, chicken, or tofu dishes.

1 cup water
2 teaspoons grated peeled fresh ginger
¼ teaspoon salt
1 (14-ounce) can fat-free, lower-sodium chicken broth
1 cup long-grain parboiled rice (such as Uncle Ben's)
¼ cup slivered almonds, toasted
¼ cup sliced green onions

1. Bring first 4 ingredients to a boil in a medium saucepan. Stir in rice; reduce heat, and simmer, covered, 18 minutes or until rice is tender and liquid is absorbed. Fluff with a fork. Stir in almonds and green onions. **YIELD:** 6 servings (serving size: ½ cup).

PER SERVING: CAL 169; FAT 2.9g (sat 0.3g); PRO 4.5g; CARB 30.4g; FIB 1.7g; SUG 0.9g; CHOL 0mg; IRON 2.3mg; SOD 285mg; CALC 36mg

desserts

Satisfy your sweet tooth with these luscious cookies, cakes, pastries, puddings, and frosty treats.

Graham Cracker Chocolate Chip Cookies

***PointsPlus* value:** 2

PREP: 12 minutes ■ **COOK:** 11 minutes per batch ■ **OTHER:** 20 minutes

Place graham crackers in a large heavy-duty zip-top plastic bag, and lightly pound with a rolling pin until crushed into large pieces.

- 1 (14-ounce) can sweetened condensed milk
- 1 teaspoon vanilla extract
- Dash of salt
- 4½ cups coarsely crushed low-fat graham crackers (about 16 cookie sheets)
- ½ cup dark chocolate chips (such as Hershey's)
- ½ cup chopped walnuts

1. Preheat oven to 350°.
2. Combine first 3 ingredients in a medium bowl. Stir in graham cracker crumbs, chocolate chips, and walnuts. Drop cracker mixture by heaping tablespoonfuls onto parchment paper–lined baking sheets.
3. Bake in batches at 350° for 11 minutes or until lightly browned. Cool cookies on pans 3 minutes. Remove cookies to a wire rack; cool completely. **YIELD:** 35 cookies (serving size: 1 cookie).

PER SERVING: CAL 70; FAT 3.1g (sat 1.3g); PRO 1.5g; CARB 9.7g; FIB 0.4g; SUG 8.5g; CHOL 3.9mg; IRON 0.1mg; SOD 31mg; CALC 40mg

Lavender Shortbread

PointsPlus **value:** 5

PREP: 5 minutes ■ **COOK:** 25 minutes

Fragrant lavender adds a special twist to this traditional cookie. Find it in the produce department in sealed plastic bags or on the baking aisle among dried herbs and spices.

6 tablespoons unsalted butter, softened
1 cup all-purpose flour
½ cup powdered sugar
¾ teaspoon dried lavender (such as Melissa's)
⅛ teaspoon salt
1 tablespoon ice water
Cooking spray
1 tablespoon granulated sugar

1. Preheat oven to 350°.
2. Place butter in a medium bowl; beat with a mixer at medium speed until light and fluffy.
3. Lightly spoon flour into a dry measuring cup; level with a knife. Combine flour and next 3 ingredients in a medium bowl; stir well with a whisk. Gradually add flour mixture to butter, beating until well blended. Add 1 tablespoon water; stir just until moist (do not overmix).
4. Press dough into an 8-inch round cake pan coated with cooking spray. Sprinkle top with granulated sugar.
5. Bake at 350° for 25 minutes or until golden brown. Score shortbread to form 8 wedges. Remove round of shortbread from pan; cool completely on a wire rack. Gently separate into individual wedges. **YIELD:** 8 servings (serving size: 1 wedge).

PER SERVING: CAL 168; FAT 8.7g (sat 5.4g); PRO 1.7g; CARB 21g; FIB 0.4g; SUG 8.8g; CHOL 23mg; IRON 0.8mg; SOD 38mg; CALC 7mg

Lavender

Lavender is a beautifully aromatic spice that comes from the mint family and adds a mysterious flavor to baked goods. As the spice dries, the aroma grows stronger, so dried lavender is stronger than the fresh variety. Since it is so pungent, be sure to use it only in small amounts.

Hazelnut-Sugar Cookie S'mores

PointsPlus **value:** 4

PREP: 10 minutes ■ **COOK:** 2 minutes

In this takeoff of the campfire classic, we replaced the customary graham crackers with sugar cookies. We slathered them with chocolate-hazelnut spread, sprinkled them with dried apricots and hazelnuts, and, of course, sandwiched them with marshmallows.

2 tablespoons chocolate-hazelnut spread (such as Nutella)
8 rectangular sugar cookies (such as Pepperidge Farm Bordeaux)
2 tablespoons finely chopped dried apricots
16 miniature marshmallows
4 teaspoons chopped hazelnuts, toasted

1. Spread ½ tablespoon chocolate-hazelnut spread on each of 4 cookies; sprinkle each with ½ tablespoon apricots and 4 marshmallows. Place on a microwave-safe plate; microwave at HIGH 20 seconds or until marshmallows puff. Sprinkle evenly with hazelnuts, and top with remaining cookies. **YIELD:** 4 servings (serving size: 1 s'more).

PER SERVING: CAL 150; FAT 6.7g (sat 2.2g); PRO 2.3g; CARB 20.8g; FIB 1.3g; SUG 15.1g; CHOL 5mg; IRON 0.7mg; SOD 54mg; CALC 15mg

Hazelnut–Sugar Cookie S'mores

Brownie Bites

Brownie Bites

PointsPlus **value:** 2

PREP: 5 minutes ■ **COOK:** 8 minutes ■ **OTHER:** 10 minutes

Cocoa nibs, which are broken bits of husked cocoa beans, add delicate chocolate flavor and delicious nutty crunch to baked goods. You can find cocoa nibs at upscale supermarkets and gourmet cookware stores. When you make this recipe, don't be alarmed that the batter is very wet—the end result will be moist, tender minicakes.

½ cup self-rising flour
⅔ cup sugar
3 tablespoons unsweetened cocoa
4 large egg whites
2 tablespoons canola oil
3 tablespoons chocolate liqueur (optional)
⅓ cup cocoa nibs
Cooking spray
Roasted salted almonds (such as Blue Diamond), coarsely chopped (optional)
Powdered sugar (optional)

1. Preheat oven to 400°.
2. Lightly spoon flour into a dry measuring cup; level with a knife. Combine flour, sugar, and cocoa in a medium bowl, stirring with a whisk.
3. Whisk egg whites until foamy in a separate bowl. Add oil and liqueur, if desired, stirring with a whisk. Add egg white mixture to flour mixture, stirring just until moist. Fold in cocoa nibs. Spoon batter evenly into 24 miniature muffin cups coated with cooking spray. Sprinkle batter evenly with almonds, if desired.
4. Bake at 400° for 8 minutes. Remove from pans; cool on wire racks. Sprinkle with powdered sugar, if desired. **YIELD:** 24 servings (serving size: 1 brownie bite).

PER SERVING: CAL 61; FAT 2.4g (sat 0.8g); PRO 1.2g; CARB 8.8g; FIB 0.3g; SUG 5.6g; CHOL 0mg; IRON 0.4mg; SOD 43mg; CALC 15mg

Chocolate Pretzel Bark

PointsPlus **value:** 5

PREP: 6 minutes ■ **COOK:** 1 minute ■ **OTHER:** 20 minutes

In less than 30 minutes, this recipe nets you a fantastic dessert or homemade gift.

12 ounces semisweet chocolate chips (such as Ghirardelli)
2 cups thin salted pretzel sticks
¾ cup chopped dried sweet cherries
½ cup chopped pistachios
¼ cup chopped crystallized ginger

1. Place chocolate in a microwave-safe bowl. Microwave at HIGH 1 to 2 minutes or until melted, stirring after 30 seconds. Stir in pretzel sticks, coarsely chopping with a wooden spoon. Pour mixture into a 13 x 9–inch baking dish lined with wax paper, spreading to coat bottom of dish. Sprinkle remaining ingredients evenly on top, pressing into chocolate mixture. Refrigerate until hardened (about 20 minutes). Invert chocolate bark onto plate; carefully peel off wax paper. Cut into 16 pieces. **YIELD:** about 1½ pounds (serving size: 1 piece).

PER SERVING: CAL 175; FAT 8g (sat 4g); PRO 2.3g; CARB 25.8g; FIB 2.4g; SUG 16.2g; CHOL 0mg; IRON 1.4mg; SOD 130mg; CALC 21mg

Flourless Chocolate Cakes

Flourless Chocolate Cakes

***PointsPlus* value:** 4

PREP: 10 minutes ■ **COOK:** 10 minutes
OTHER: 10 minutes

With rich chocolate flavor and a warm gooey filling, these hot-from-the-oven minicakes are the perfect indulgence at the end of a busy day. Many supermarkets stock ground pecans in the nuts section; if you can't find them already ground, chop pecan halves or pieces, and grind them in a food processor, minichopper, or spice grinder.

1 large egg
¼ cup sugar
2 teaspoons unsweetened cocoa
1½ tablespoons chopped pecans, ground
1 tablespoon warm water
1 ounce bittersweet chocolate, melted and cooled slightly
Cooking spray
Powdered sugar (optional)
Strawberries (optional)

1. Preheat oven to 425°.
2. Separate egg, placing egg white and egg yolk in separate medium bowls. Add sugar and cocoa to egg yolk, stirring with a whisk. Add pecans, 1 tablespoon water, and chocolate, stirring with a whisk.
3. Beat egg white with a mixer at high speed until stiff peaks form. Gently fold half of egg white into egg yolk mixture; fold in remaining egg white. Spoon batter evenly into 4 (4-ounce) ramekins coated with cooking spray.
4. Bake at 425° for 10 minutes or until almost set. Transfer to a wire rack; cool 10 minutes. Garnish with powdered sugar and strawberries, if desired. **YIELD:** 4 servings (serving size: 1 ramekin).

PER SERVING: CAL 124; FAT 6.2g (sat 2.1g); PRO 2.5g; CARB 17.3g; FIB 1.1g; SUG 15.5g; CHOL 45mg; IRON 0.6mg; SOD 18mg; CALC 10mg

Cocoa Powder

Cocoa powder is made from ground roasted cacao seeds that have had most of the fat removed. When you are using less real chocolate in light baking, incorporate some cocoa powder to deepen the chocolate flavor without adding a lot of extra fat.

Brandied Pear Pastries with Apricot Glaze

***PointsPlus* value:** 3

PREP: 7 minutes ■ **COOK:** 20 minutes

Serve these slightly sweet tarts warm with fat-free vanilla ice cream or at room temperature all by themselves. Be sure your pears are tender ripe so they'll cook by the time the pastry is golden.

½ (17.3-ounce) package frozen puff pastry dough, thawed
Butter-flavored cooking spray
¼ cup apricot fruit spread (such as Polaner All Fruit)
2 cups sliced peeled ripe Anjou pear (2 small pears)
1 tablespoon brandy
1 tablespoon sliced almonds

1. Preheat oven to 400°.
2. Roll pastry dough into a 12-inch square on a baking sheet lined with parchment paper; cut pastry into 12 (3 x 4–inch) rectangles. Pierce each rectangle with a fork. Coat dough with cooking spray.
3. Place fruit spread in a small microwave-safe bowl. Microwave at HIGH 30 seconds or until melted.
4. Arrange pear slices evenly on top of rectangles. Brush pear slices with brandy. Brush pear slices and pastry with fruit spread. Sprinkle with almonds. Bake at 400° for 20 minutes or until pear is tender and pastry is golden. **YIELD:** 12 servings (serving size: 1 pastry).

PER SERVING: CAL 118; FAT 6g (sat 1.5g); PRO 1.7g; CARB 14g; FIB 1.2g; SUG 5.5g; CHOL 0mg; IRON 0.6mg; SOD 100mg; CALC 14mg

Apple-Cranberry Galette

***PointsPlus* value:** 4
PREP: 8 minutes ■ **COOK:** 35 minutes

Cranberries provide tiny tart bursts of flavor and bright color in this sweet rustic apple pie.

½ (14.1-ounce) package refrigerated pie dough (such as Pillsbury)
Butter-flavored cooking spray
¼ cup sugar, divided
½ teaspoon ground cinnamon
5 cups sliced peeled Golden Delicious apple (about 4 apples)
½ cup frozen cranberries, thawed

1. Preheat oven to 400°.
2. Roll dough into a 12-inch circle; place on a baking sheet coated with cooking spray.
3. Combine 3 tablespoons sugar and cinnamon in a large bowl. Add apple and cranberries, stirring to coat with sugar mixture. Spoon apple mixture onto crust, leaving a 2-inch border. Fold dough over filling, forming a 2-inch border of dough that partially covers filling. Press gently to seal. Coat dough with cooking spray, and sprinkle with 1 tablespoon sugar.
4. Bake at 400° for 35 minutes or until apple is tender and crust is golden. Let galette cool slightly on pan before cutting. **YIELD:** 10 servings (serving size: 1 wedge).

PER SERVING: CAL 155; FAT 5.4g (sat 2.2g); PRO 1g; CARB 26.7g; FIB 1.5g; SUG 15.1g; CHOL 4mg; IRON 0.1mg; SOD 74mg; CALC 6mg

Triple-Chocolate Pudding

***PointsPlus* value:** 5
PREP: 5 minutes ■ **COOK:** 12 minutes ■ **OTHER:** 5 minutes

Modest in appearance yet boasting an intense flavor and a made-from-scratch taste, this simple, satisfying chocolate pudding is the quintessential weeknight dessert. Place plastic wrap on the surface of the hot pudding to prevent a skin from forming during chilling.

1 (5-ounce) package chocolate cook-and-serve pudding mix
1 large egg yolk
4 cups 1% low-fat chocolate milk
1 ounce semisweet chocolate, chopped
1 teaspoon vanilla extract
Frozen reduced-calorie whipped topping, thawed (optional)
Semisweet chocolate shavings (optional)

1. Combine first 3 ingredients in a medium saucepan. Bring to a boil over medium heat, stirring constantly with a whisk. Boil 2 minutes, stirring constantly. Remove from heat. Add chopped chocolate and vanilla, stirring with a whisk until chocolate melts. Cool 5 minutes.
2. Spoon ½ cup pudding into each of 8 individual serving bowls. Serve warm, or cover surface of pudding with plastic wrap, and chill thoroughly. Top each serving with whipped topping, if desired; sprinkle with chocolate shavings, if desired. **YIELD:** 8 servings (serving size: 1 pudding).

PER SERVING: CAL 169; FAT 2.8g (sat 1.6g); PRO 5.2g; CARB 31.3g; FIB 0.7g; SUG 12.7g; CHOL 31mg; IRON 0.7mg; SOD 187mg; CALC 151mg

Triple-Chocolate Pudding

White Chocolate–Cherry
Rice Pudding

White Chocolate-Cherry Rice Pudding

***PointsPlus* value:** 4
PREP: 4 minutes ■ **COOK:** 7 minutes

When you're looking for a quick dessert, turn to this superfast pudding that's spiced with ground cinnamon and flecked with cherries. This shortcut method of using an instant pudding mix delivers that characteristic creamy texture of rice pudding without the long cooking time.

3½ cups 1% low-fat milk, divided
⅓ cup dried cherries
2 tablespoons light brown sugar
¼ teaspoon ground cinnamon
1 tablespoon butter
⅛ teaspoon salt
1 cup instant rice
1 (1-ounce) package sugar-free white chocolate instant pudding mix
Cinnamon sticks (optional)

1. Bring 1½ cups milk, dried cherries, and next 4 ingredients to a boil in a medium saucepan over medium heat, stirring occasionally. Stir in rice; cover and reduce heat to low. Simmer 5 minutes, stirring occasionally.
2. While rice mixture cooks, prepare pudding mix according to package directions using remaining 2 cups milk. Stir prepared pudding into rice mixture. Serve warm. Garnish with cinnamon sticks, if desired. **YIELD:** 8 servings (serving size: ½ cup).

PER SERVING: CAL 156; FAT 2.6g (sat 1.6g); PRO 5g; CARB 27.9g; FIB 0.7g; SUG 12.1g; CHOL 8mg; IRON 0.9mg; SOD 141mg; CALC 142mg

Chocolate-Peppermint Parfaits

***PointsPlus* value:** 5
PREP: 8 minutes

You'll love the contrasting textures of the crisp meringue cookies and peppermints with the velvety ice cream.

1 cup coarsely chopped vanilla meringue cookies (such as Miss Meringue; about 4 cookies)
2 cups chocolate light ice cream (such as Edy's)
1 cup refrigerated canned light whipped topping (such as Reddi-wip)
½ cup finely crushed soft peppermint candies

1. Spoon ¼ cup cookies into each of 4 parfait glasses; top each serving with ¼ cup ice cream, 2 tablespoons whipped topping, and 1 tablespoon peppermint candies. Repeat layers with remaining ice cream, whipped topping, and peppermint candies. **YIELD:** 4 servings (serving size: 1 parfait).

PER SERVING: CAL 222; FAT 4g (sat 2g); PRO 2.1g; CARB 39.3g; FIB 0g; SUG 19.1g; CHOL 11mg; IRON 0.4mg; SOD 57mg; CALC 80mg

Sweet Potato-Gingersnap Parfaits

***PointsPlus* value:** 4
PREP: 5 minutes

For this easy stir-together dessert, you can use canned sweet potato, or bake and mash a medium-size sweet potato.

1 cup canned sweet potato casserole (such as Glory)
¼ cup crème fraîche
1 tablespoon light maple-flavored syrup (such as Aunt Jemima)
2 cups frozen fat-free whipped topping, thawed and divided
¼ cup crunchy honey-almond flax cereal (such as Kashi GoLean)
1 tablespoon chopped crystallized ginger
3 gingersnaps, coarsely crumbled

1. Combine first 3 ingredients in a medium bowl, mashing with a fork. Gently fold in 1½ cups whipped topping. Spoon mixture evenly into 6 parfait glasses or small dessert dishes; top evenly with ½ cup whipped topping.
2. Place cereal, ginger, and cookie crumbs in a mini chopper; pulse 4 times or until crumbs are uniform. Sprinkle cereal mixture evenly over desserts. Chill, if desired. **YIELD:** 6 servings (serving size: 1 parfait).

PER SERVING: CAL 148; FAT 2.2g (sat 1.1g); PRO 1.5g; CARB 29g; FIB 1.1g; SUG 13.8g; CHOL 4mg; IRON 0.4mg; SOD 136mg; CALC 17mg

Apple Pie Scoops

***PointsPlus* value:** 7

PREP: 5 minutes ■ **COOK:** 13 minutes

This dessert is essentially a deconstructed applesauce pie. Cooking the "filling" separately from the crust shaves off loads of time. Use the crisp, spiced strips to scoop up the applesauce.

½ (15-ounce) package refrigerated pie dough (such as Pillsbury)
Butter-flavored cooking spray
4 teaspoons bottled cinnamon sugar, divided
1 (24-ounce) jar chunky applesauce (such as Musselman's)
1 tablespoon brown sugar
2 teaspoons butter
6 tablespoons vanilla fat-free ice cream (optional)

1. Preheat oven to 425°.
2. Cover a large baking sheet with parchment paper; secure with masking tape. Roll pie dough into a 12-inch circle on parchment paper. Pierce entire surface liberally with a fork. With a pastry wheel or sharp knife, cut dough into 3 x 1–inch strips. Lightly coat strips with cooking spray; sprinkle evenly with 2 teaspoons cinnamon sugar. Bake at 425° for 13 minutes or until golden brown.
3. While dough strips bake, combine applesauce, remaining 2 teaspoons cinnamon sugar, brown sugar, and butter in a medium saucepan. Place over medium heat; cook 6 minutes or until sugars dissolve, stirring occasionally.
4. Spoon applesauce into each of 6 serving dishes. Top each serving with 1 tablespoon ice cream, if desired, and serve with cinnamon strips. **YIELD:** 6 servings (serving size: about ½ cup applesauce mixture and 8 scoops).

PER SERVING: CAL 263; FAT 10.6g (sat 4.2g); PRO 1.4g; CARB 42.5g; FIB 2.2g; SUG 22.3g; CHOL 3.4mg; IRON 0.1mg; SOD 205mg; CALC 11mg

Banana-Caramel Sundaes

***PointsPlus* value:** 7

PREP: 8 minutes

Candy-coated almonds give this super fast, simple ice-cream sundae a little something extra special. For variety, try substituting your favorite sugared or candied nut for the almonds.

2 large bananas
1⅓ cups vanilla low-fat ice cream
¼ cup fat-free caramel topping (such as Smucker's)
⅓ cup chopped cinnamon-coated almonds

1. Cut each banana in half crosswise and then in half lengthwise to make 8 quarters. Place 2 banana quarters in each of 4 stemmed glasses or 4 individual serving bowls. Top each serving with ⅓ cup ice cream and 1 tablespoon caramel topping; sprinkle each serving with about 1 tablespoon almonds. **YIELD:** 4 servings (serving size: 1 sundae).

PER SERVING: CAL 255; FAT 5g (sat 1.7g); PRO 3.8g; CARB 49.1g; FIB 2.6g; SUG 34.2g; CHOL 12mg; IRON 0.5mg; SOD 100mg; CALC 90mg

Candy-Coated Almonds

Cinnamon-coated almonds are great to use for embellishing recipes that only call for a few ingredients. Try them on desserts such as ice-cream sundaes or as an addition to sweet-and-savory recipes such as salads. Look for the almonds either with the other nuts in your supermarket or near the produce section.

Banana-Caramel
Sundaes

ABOUT OUR RECIPES

Each recipe in the *Weight Watchers Five Ingredient 15 Minute Recipes* has a complete list of nutrients—including calories, fat, saturated fat, protein, carbohydrates, dietary fiber, sugar, cholesterol, iron, sodium, and calcium—as well as a serving size and the yield. Measurements are abbreviated g (grams) and mg (milligrams). Nutritional values either come from The Food Processor, Version 7.5 (ESHA Research), or are provided by food manufacturers. Numbers are based on these assumptions:

• Unless otherwise indicated in the ingredient list, servings of meat, poultry, and fish always refer to skinned, boned, and cooked servings.

• When we give a range in the amount for an ingredient, we calculate the nutrients using the lesser amount listed.

• Some alcohol calories evaporate during heating; the analysis reflects this.

• Only the amount of marinade absorbed by the food is used in calculations.

• Garnishes and optional ingredients are not included in an analysis.

Sodium: The latest recommendation for sodium intake in the *Dietary Guidelines for Americans, 2005* is less than 2,300 mg of sodium (approximately 1 teaspoon salt) per day. Decreasing sodium is a challenge in quick-cooking recipes because so many convenience products are high in sodium. In this cookbook, we've tried to keep the sodium as low as possible while still maintaining great flavor. However, some of the recipes may be too high in sodium for people on a strict low-sodium diet. Every recipe has a sodium value, so you'll be able to select the ones that work best for you.

Diabetic Exchanges: We have stopped including Diabetic Exchanges with the recipes because most dietitians and diabetes educators are now teaching people with diabetes to count total carbohydrates at each meal and snack, rather than counting exchanges. Counting carbohydrates provides more flexibility in one's food choices and seems to be effective in managing blood glucose. Almost all of our recipes can be built into a diabetic diet by incorporating the carbohydrate amount in the nutrient analysis into the carbohydrate amount recommended by your physician.

Safety Note: Cooking spray should never be used near direct heat. Always remove a pan from heat before coating it with cooking spray.

PointsPlus® VALUE INDEX

PointsPlus® VALUE INDEX

***PointsPlus* VALUE: 8**

***PointsPlus* VALUE: 9**

***PointsPlus* VALUE: 10**

RECIPE INDEX

🔴 family favorites 🔵 make ahead 🟢 no cook 🟡 portable

APPETIZERS, SNACKS & BEVERAGES

BEVERAGES

DESSERTS

FISH & SHELLFISH

MEATLESS MAIN DISHES

MEATS (BEEF, LAMB, PORK)

POULTRY

SALADS

SANDWICHES

SIDES

RECIPE INDEX

● family favorites ● make ahead ● no cook ● portable

METRIC EQUIVALENTS

Liquid Ingredients by Volume

¼ tsp							=	1 ml
½ tsp							=	2 ml
1 tsp							=	5 ml
3 tsp	=	1 tbl			=	½ fl oz	=	15 ml
		2 tbls	=	⅛ cup	=	1 fl oz	=	30 ml
		4 tbls	=	¼ cup	=	2 fl oz	=	60 ml
		5⅓ tbls	=	⅓ cup	=	3 fl oz	=	80 ml
		8 tbls	=	½ cup	=	4 fl oz	=	120 ml
		10⅔ tbls	=	⅔ cup	=	5 fl oz	=	160 ml
		12 tbls	=	¾ cup	=	6 fl oz	=	180 ml
		16 tbls	=	1 cup	=	8 fl oz	=	240 ml
		1 pt	=	2 cups	=	16 fl oz	=	480 ml
		1 qt	=	4 cups	=	32 fl oz	=	960 ml
						33 fl oz	=	1000 ml = 1 l

Dry Ingredients by Weight

(To convert ounces to grams, multiply the number of ounces by 30.)

1 oz	=	1/16 lb	=	30 g
4 oz	=	¼ lb	=	120 g
8 oz	=	½ lb	=	240 g
12 oz	=	¾ lb	=	360 g
16 oz	=	1 lb	=	480 g

Equivalents for Different Types of Ingredients

Standard Cup	Fine Powder (ex. flour)	Grain (ex. rice)	Granular (ex. sugar)	Liquid Solids (ex. butter)	Liquid (ex. milk)
1	140 g	150 g	190 g	200 g	240 ml
¾	105 g	113 g	143 g	150 g	180 ml
⅔	93 g	100 g	125 g	133 g	160 ml
½	70 g	75 g	95 g	100 g	120 ml
⅓	47 g	50 g	63 g	67 g	80 ml
¼	35 g	38 g	48 g	50 g	60 ml
⅛	18 g	19 g	24 g	25 g	30 ml

Cooking/Oven Temperatures

	Fahrenheit	Celsius	Gas Mark
Freeze Water	32° F	0° C	
Room Temperature	68° F	20° C	
Boil Water	212° F	100° C	
Bake	325° F	160° C	3
	350° F	180° C	4
	375° F	190° C	5
	400° F	200° C	6
	425° F	220° C	7
	450° F	230° C	8
Broil			Grill